Scenes from a Vegetable Plot

Growing organic is *EASY!*

If one fool can do it, so can you!
No… hang on...
that doesn't seem quite right…

Chas Griffin

SCENES FROM A VEGETABLE PLOT

Published by The Good Life Press Ltd. 2011

ISBN 978 1 90487 1934

A catalogue record for this book is available from the British Library.

Published by
The Good Life Press Ltd.
The Old Pigsties
Clifton Fields
Lytham Road
Preston
PR4 0XG

www.goodlifepress.co.uk
www.homefarmer.co.uk

Contents

Foreword

Let's start with an apology... I originally wrote this little book as a no-nonsense guide for absolute beginners on how to grow organic veg in a garden or an allotment. It's easy... It really is, as you will find when you read on, and then try it for yourself.

However... what you read within won't really qualify as 'scenes', as in 'gory personal memoirs or frilly and evocative descriptions' of life on a veg plot. The book does contain lots of practical stuff gleaned from personal experience, but not a lot of...

'As I gazed across the rolling beds of gaily-tinted climbing beans and little clumps of hibiscus-flowering okra, shading my eyes against the slanting light of an August dawn, I suddenly realised that with a bit of hammering and a bodged-up slab of MDF I could probably wedge two, or maybe even three, clapped-out old battery hens into that lean-to karzi by the back wall.'

So the *Scenes* in the title is essentially fraudulent.
'Why is it there then?' you ask, and not unreasonably.
It is because of... 'The Editor'.
You will perhaps have heard writers refer to... 'The Editor' in much the same tone as backbenchers refer to 'The PM', or a child to 'The Headmaster', but possibly with a little less fear or despair.

The thing is, The Editor has the power to pull the plug, and must thus be carefully listened to. An Editor is not necessarily the enemy of style or truth (though this may be the case, I'm sad to say), but can tidy stuff up, corect spellings, and shuffle material about for better effect.

They are also deeply concerned with marketing, which, as everyone who has ever tried to sell anything (from a clapped-out Metro to the last wellington on the stall) knows to be a very tricky job indeed. Books are incredibly hard to market, as the competition is fierce. It's not a question of 'the hard sell' here, but simply of getting the book noticed *at all*, amidst the literally 150,000 or more titles released every year (that's over 400 a *day*). Publishers pay a solid whack of money to Waterstone's to have their own books stacked on a table near the door. The more favourable the position on the table, the more they pay. Bet you didn't know that, did you? It's *that* competitive.

So...

The two most important things to tempt someone into picking up a book are an eye-catching cover, and the title. Did you, Modom (or esteemed Sir), pick this book up because of the cover or the title? If it was the cover, that will be partly down to Ken Guy who drew the cartoon. If, on the other hand, it was the title that beguiled and tempted you, then that is down to Ruth Tott, who is (hushed intake of breath...) 'The Editor'.

I originally wanted to call the book *The Organic Plotter*, but my wife didn't like it much, and frankly neither did I, but I couldn't think of anything better.

The Editor immediately suggested *Scenes from...*, as a marketing ploy, hoping to attract the attention of the massed scores of people who have enjoyed my previous books, *Scenes from a Smallholding* and *More Scenes from a Smallholding*. Clever stuff, but just one problem. There were no 'scenes' in the text.

OK, I puffed, I'll add some, and went away to think... and think...

...and...

...eventually realised that I simply didn't *have* any suitable personal stuff that would count as 'scenes'. Pretty well all my memories had either gone into the two previous books, or were already condensed into the present text.

However, I did still have a few more smallholding experiences to draw upon, so I've just dropped one or two of them in here and there, hoping that The Editor won't notice that they are largely irrelevant to the problems of a back-yard gardener who needs wise words on the best way to get a mouse out of the spout of a watering-can (Deep breath: and *blow*; failing that, fill the can and gently slosh it about; if desperate, a bottle-brush dipped in ammonia), or sensible advice on how to minimise blight on their potato crop (see Chapter 8).

So... with any luck, this disclaimer will satisfy all parties, and might at the very least stop The Editor from being sued for knowingly marketing an unfit title.

Yes... 'The Editor'... 'It was all her idea. Nothing to do with me, m'lud. So har har. Send her *dahn*, m'lud... off to the hulks... Botany Bay's too good for 'er...'

Anyway, I do hope you enjoy this present '*Scenes*'. Growing organic food really *is* easy, if you're prepared to think and pay attention; and the fact that you've got this far down this page proves that you have the persistence and sheer stamina that will stand you in excellent stead when faced with a bullock in the lettuce patch, and slugs abseiling down from a windowsill onto your pansies. Don't laugh. They've both happened to me, and may, of course, happen to you.

The good news is that once you are working with Nature, you will find a way to smile at both bullock and the slugs. Guaranteed.

Oh... and right at the end I've added a longish chapter of what I think might be handy tips for anyone who gets inspired enough by the wonders of gardening to step up a gear and try smallholding. We tried it and loved it, bullocks and all.

All best wishes,

CG.

Chapter 1
Why? Why? And Where?

Congratulations! You have chosen sanity! Not just because you are clearly interested in how to grow proper food at a proper price that actually does you good instead of slowly killing you... *but*... also because you have chosen to embark on a path that will bring you endless fun, happiness, joy, well-being, and if you get it right... endless strawberries too. Yes... endless *strawberries*... and new potatoes... and asparagus... and fresh sweetcorn... Mmmm...

This is only a slim volume as there is actually very little to say about growing vegetables, especially organically. It's really very easy indeed. It only looks hard to a beginner because there is a huge publishing and television industry devoted to making it look difficult so it can sell you more and more glossy books and DVDs and interactive 5-dimensional presentations in 64 million colours.

All you actually need to get going is this little book and a dollop of common sense. Forget the experts. Just get on with it.
Right.. let's do that:
This chapter is about Why Gardening? Why Organic? and Where do you do it?

Why Gardening?

It is a truth universally acknowledged that nobody in the entire history of the universe has ever seen an angry gardener. That's because gardening is good for the soul. It engages you, not just with a job that is worthwhile, but also with the rhythms of Nature, as opposed to a modern office job where you don't even have a freshly shuffled pile of paper to show for a day's wasted life. And all too often, a Day At The Paperless Office ends with *Tippex* dabs on the monitor screen and a canvas jacket to go home in, as we all know.
In a garden you can *see* the results of your labour, and it is good. A pattern of pansies or a patch of burgeoning lettuce

seedlings, freshly watered in, satisfies our creative urges, which have been all but knocked out of us in this over-consumerised and passiv-icated age. We *need* to be creative, and gardening is a wonderfully efficient way of engaging our creative urges; organic gardening even more so. And now that heightened sensibility has taken peacock off the menu, nothing satisfies the old hunter-gatherer in us better than a hatful of zinging-fresh peas.

Of course, it does depend on what sort of gardening you are going in for. Razored lawns and anally retentive conical topiary will do you no good at all, but something freewheeling and a little curvy will bring you and everyone else endless delight. Some people seem to think that if a garden is not planned according to military standards of rectitude and angularity then it can't be efficient. Not true. Nature does pretty well for efficiency and beauty too, with never a straight line in sight.

So should you not plan your garden? Just let it find its own way?

No... you definitely should plan it carefully if you want to avoid disease and pests. The art lies in hiding the art. Sometimes straight lines; sometimes not, but always with pest avoidance in mind (see Chapter 7).

Working in a garden calms the mind and the emotions. By focussing on a single physical task you immediately push aside the worries and frustrations that we are normally prone to. Add to this the fact that the jobs you are doing are often matters of life and death (plants have lives too, you know...) and you find that your emotions become engaged in acts of caring, and you actively want to do the best you can for these little creatures in the soil before you.

Over-romantic? Not at all. We all have an instinct for caring but have largely forgotten how broadly we can use it. And it is a truth not yet universally acknowledged, that the more care you give out, the happier you will feel. Caring is healthy.

What's more, on a purely practical level, whether you like it or not, your food (*all* your food) ultimately comes from seeds and plants which somebody somewhere has sown into the earth. The plants they carefully sowed may have been fed to an animal, but eventually the essence of the plant, which some stranger somewhere once put into the soil, lands up on your plate, as a salad or a rogan josh. You are very intimately connected with the produce of the earth and the care that went into getting it to your door. I'm amazed at how many people don't know this fact. If they did know it, and knew how much work and care goes into producing their food, they would never waste a single crust. As it is, we in the UK currently waste an estimated £7.3 *billion* worth of food every year. This represents some 300,000 *tons* of food, in a world where millions are starving. Some would regard that as not merely scandalous, but obscene. Whatever, it is highly indicative of how remote most of us have become from how our food is produced. But you're about to change all that, aren't you? Excellent.

In deciding to produce at least some of our own food we are doing what Man (and 'Woman', yes, alright...) was meant to do... to work with the land to earn our *living*, as opposed to clawing in ever-greater virtual mounds of digital dosh to spend on things that don't actually make us happy. We live on *food*, not dividends or playing computer games or buying sixteen different i-Pods.

And I tell you as a fact... you will never taste a better onion than one you've grown yourself. This is literally true for several reasons which I hope will become obvious.

So The Answer to the Question Why Gardening? Is:

'For the sake of your own enjoyment, sanity, and blood pressure; to satisfy your much neglected creative needs; and to grow better food than you can buy, at a fraction of the cost of the rubbish in the supermarkets. And oh yes... it's terrific exercise too. Forget the stinking gym: what you need isn't consumerised and computerised 'work-outs'; it's productive, enjoyable.. *creative effort.*'

Why Organic?

This section is designed to point out the dangers of 'chemical' food production, and to forcefully underline why we should all grow organic food instead: gardeners, allotmenteers, growers, farmers...

Some of what follows may surprise or even shock you. Whatever, I hope it will encourage you even more to get stuck in, and grow at least some of your own healthy food.

There are two main reasons for growing organically: health and sustainability.

There have been scores of studies done which indicate very powerfully that children brought up on organic food are healthier and happier than kids dragged up on junk food. They thus perform better at school, even to the point of developing higher IQs. This is no surprise to anyone except just about everyone in government. Governments all seem to be immune to what these researches show. Instead of doing the obvious thing and going all-out to support organic agriculture to correct some of the harm we are doing to our next generation, they would rather keep taxing us to pay for extra probation officers, police, hospital staff, and psychiatrists to cope with thousands of damaged kids whose only problem is the crap they eat. Cut the crap and cut the costs. And en route you have a generation of happier children, less crime, less drug dependency, fewer self-harmings and suicides... You can add to this list at your leisure.

Jamie Oliver has made heroic efforts, but the crap food culture has been so battered into us by the Advertisers and their shadowy allies the Free Market Economists, and of course Big Business, that ignorant Mums across the land see no harm in crisps and Red Bull as a main course for their toddlers. Can you see the future looming?

We are, quite literally, what we eat. There can be no disputing that. If you stuff your child with additives, colourisers, preservatives, extra salt (to give the rubbish some semblance of taste), extra sugar (to go straight to the comfort zone of someone sub-clinically depressed), not to mention 'enhancers', 'preservatives', 'stabilisers', 'pink fairy dust', and God knows what else... well, I guess you can see what I'm getting at. ALL those things are factory-manufactured chemicals*. And people, particularly young people, still developing in mind and body, are NOT designed to live on chemicals.

Your children need top quality food. That means 'organically grown food' untainted by any artificial chemical.

The chemicals in 'normal' (ie 'chemically-grown') food are not limited to the stack of additives in the processed junk so many poor kids are stuffed with.

Chemical procedures are endemic to the whole of the farming and growing industry. By and large, people don't know what goes on down on the farm. Forget rosy-cheeked piglets and merry apple pickers with battered hats and cheery grins. Think huge tractors with enormous booms spraying nerve toxins onto what will end up in a multi-wrapped plastic tray labelled *Nature's Loveliest Spring Bounty*, complete with a picture of rosy-cheeked piglets in battered hats etc, on a supermarket shelf.

Crops will not just be sprayed to destroy or control a known and actual pest, but (and again, not many people know this) they may also be sprayed several times as a pre-emptive against a *possible* pest attack. Perfectly healthy plants, sprayed again and again with poisonous chemicals...

What's more, peas, for example, are likely to be sprayed with a noxious chemical so that the vine will wither quicker, thus enabling easier harvesting.

Unless the food you buy is clearly labelled 'Organic', it will certainly have been subjected to various chemical treatments, sometimes at a grotesque level. One Dutch lettuce producer was prosecuted for treating his crop with no fewer than 28 doses of pesticide. Does this ever happen elsewhere? How do we know? And anyway, how much pesticide is 'safe'? Every now and then another batch of poisons is banned. Yesterday they were 'perfectly safe, ha-ha, don't worry your pretty little head about it, dear'; today, apparently, they are not. Who decides? How? People used to commit suicide in the UK by drinking paraquat, the weed killer of choice for lawn freaks: it was 'safe'. Now it's banned, but not across the world. It's still popular for suicides among farmers ruined by Big Aggro-Business Corporations in the third world.

Pesticides kill pesty insects, but also a lot of friendly insects vital to Nature's food chain and to keeping other pests under control. And, of course, via the path of Natural Selection, the pests gradually develop resistance; hence the need for ever more toxic poisons. But don't worry your pretty little etc, etc...

Perhaps most importantly of all, pesticides kill bees... probably the most important insect in the world from the human point of view, as they pollinate so many of our crops for us. No bees = no pollination. No pollination = no crops. No crops = ...

Fungicides kill various moulds which can damage crops. Right. But what harm might they also be doing to the micro-fungi which are essential to a healthy soil? A teaspoon of healthy soil contains literally billions of tiny lives, all symbiotically existing, and enabling the healthy growth of the plants we depend upon to live. Soil is powdered rock, plus rotted organic matter, plus billions of tiny critters which break down the rotting stuff and make it available as recycled food to the plants. If you kill off these tiny lives, you end up with barren rock dust; nothing will grow in it. The soil is dead. And shortly after, so are we. Soil Death is actually an enormous crisis in the making which no government I've heard of has even acknowledged the existence of as yet. We'll be hearing of it shortly however, you may be sure of that.

On the subject of chemicals, we all know what a fertiliser is, don't we? It is something that feeds a plant. A plant is a small life, in some ways similar to a puppy or a toddler, but with more leaves. You would never dream of raising a pup or a baby on chemical food; why would you do the same to a seedling? You know that it, like any other small creature needs proper natural food, which means highly complex organic material.

If you've ever seen ghastly lanky and clearly distressed cabbage or lettuce seedlings in a tray outside a shop, you know instinctively there's something wrong with them. Of course there is... they've been reared on chemical fertiliser.

'Fertiliser' to an organic gardener means 'compost', of which more in Chapter 3.

There's more... **Please don't feel obliged to read the next paragraph or two, but if you do you will understand better why organic growers are passionate about their job.**

Pesticides... fungicides... herbicides... all powerful poisons. Taken together they are called 'biocides', meaning that they 'kill life'.

Poisons have two characteristics over and above the obvious: firstly, they are not nearly as selective as people think they ought to be. What kills a sap-sucking aphid won't be doing the aphid's predators any good either; secondly, there's the cocktail effect. Mix any two chemicals and you open up the possibility of a composite effect which might be either many times more powerful than you would expect from the known nature of the inputs, or which may have quite unexpected consequences in other directions. And NOBODY knows what the infinite number of combinations of chemicals, soil type, soil life, moisture levels, timing etc might be doing to our soil, our crops and ourselves. All we can be sure of is it ain't going to do any good in the long run, and all too likely not in the short run either.

Just by the by... DDT has been found in the fat of Antarctic penguins.

Yes, there's more. We all know how powerful hormones can be ('Put the vase down, dear...'). Does it surprise you to hear that hormones are regularly used in farming simply to promote animal growth? Some countries are stricter than others about the use of these extraordinarily potent chemicals, but as we import food from all over the world, even when we are perfectly capable of producing our own**, the smart thing to do is to assume that imported meat may have been tainted.

You do *not* 'need' food which has been in any way treated with hormones, some of which have been linked with increased risk of cancers.

The routine misuse of antibiotics as animal growth promoters has led to the emergence of antibiotic-resistant strains of *Salmonella*. Who benefits from this practice? Three guesses. Should it continue?

Radiation is used to preserve potatoes in winter stores. Does radiation do good things to living creatures, do you think? Would it be better to not irradiate food, if possible? And are you tired of being asked rhetorical questions?

Then there's Genetic Modification... There are whole books written about this. The essential point for gardeners and farmers to bear in mind is that Nature has decreed, for whatever whimsy, that cabbages and wheat should not glow in the dark. Each species of plant has a limited gene pool from which variation might develop. To insert genes for eg 'luminescence', or 'poisonous to bugs' is to court disaster, a point which is clear to anybody who has any understanding at all of the complexity of The Ecosystem (of which there is only one). It would seem that the chemical engineers who concoct these 'Frankenstein crops' have little understanding of what The Ecosystem is. Perhaps they think it just doesn't apply to them. After all, they are *Scientists,* and have thus replaced Nature... and common sense, it would seem.

Anything genetically modified or engineered should be regarded with extreme caution. Once a modification escapes it can cause untold and literally unpredictable damage. There are already 'superweeds' (some in Canada, for example) on the rampage which are immune to normal herbicides. Why? Because a GM crop was bred to be herbicide resistant, so that the weeds infesting a crop could then be sprayed with impunity. Guess what? Some weeds developed resistance (via that new-fangled thing called Natural Selection that biochemists and genetic engineers seem not to have heard of over the last 150 years) and *escaped,* as Life always does.

Remember *Jurassic Park*? Only a story, but a warning, nonetheless.

The Canadian superweed is not the only example, and more will follow as sure as night follows day, as long as we think we can mess with something we don't 100% understand. Meanwhile, beware: cross a *T Rex* with a nettle, and we're in for a very prickly time.

Have I definitely reassured you that organic is best yet?

There's more...

The reason food is so cheap (relative to our overall income) is because supermarkets have a virtual monopoly on food. Thus, they have been able to cut prices to you and me by forcing down the price they pay the farmers. This has a knock-on effect. To keep prices low, corner-cutting is encouraged, as is any other trick in the agricultural book. *All* the shop cares about is profit. I think I should repeat that, and put it in a nice little box, beautifully labelled and displayed, along with a nice picture of a rosy-cheeked pig in a pin-striped suit:

> ## ALL THAT
> Crappo Supersavers Inc.
> Is Interested In Is
> Profit

To produce the cheapest possible food, as dictated by *Crappo*, the farmer needs to grow on a large scale, and to over-stress his soil with artificial fertilisers, and to concentrate on only one crop. This is called 'monoculture' and it leads sooner or later to ecological disaster. Everybody knows this, possibly even supermarket executives, who simply don't care as long as their obscene profits keep rolling in, but not government experts, apparently, who resolutely continue to deny the ecological necessity of the organic approach.

This is how monoculture pans out: if you grow just one crop, the pests and diseases of that crop get to build up, don't they? Of course they do. But what can the poor farmer do? He can't change his crop 'just like that', as growing a new crop is a highly tricky business, believe me, and anyway *Crappo SuperSavers* has him by the throat. Where else can he sell his crop, geared up entirely to lettuces, on contract to *Crappo*? Lettuces perish in two days, and he has 50,000 on the field... with another 150,000 coming on.... as encouraged by *Crappo*.... his *'business partner'*.

All he can do is to spray his crop with ever more nasty chemicals. He will spray as a preventative, as often as he feels he must... egged on all the time by the aggro-chemical industry's friendly rep. He simply cannot afford a crop failure. He has no back-stop in the form of several other crops as his ancestors had. He *must* spray, even though he would rather not, not least because of the expense.

The next step, of course, is for the Aggro people to sell him GM seed... 'It won't need as much spraying, you see!' Oh, right... but the seed costs vastly more than normal (perfectly adequate) seed, and you will need to buy it every year, instead of keeping your own from your own crop. Also, it *will* need spraying (if the poor farmer is to make a modest profit upon which to live, given the constant and rapacious screwing from *Crappo*): 'Sorry, Farmer Tom, but the market price for spuds is down another £20 a ton this year....' Who says so? *Crappo* says so... and they should know... it's them that rig the market, via the stranglehold they have over every farmer in the land.

Convinced yet? There's more...

Given that our poor farmers are being constantly strangled by the half a dozen *Crappo Incs* that rule the country's food and nutrition, would you be surprised to learn that for every calorie of food-energy produced by the farmers, many more calories are expended in the energy needed to produce the diesel fuel for the tractors and to produce the chemical fertilisers and biocides... (and all fertilisers in 'normal' farming are made from, wait for it... oil). The energy *cost* of food far exceeds the energy *value* of the food that conventional, chemical, farming can produce. Guess what will *definitely* happen to the price of food when the price of oil rockets through the roof, as it will one day fairly soon?

Oil is an absolutely limited resource. One day it *will* give out completely. The only question is 'when'? Twenty years? Fifty? What happens then? A child of five can answer that one, assuming it isn't roaring round the ceiling, high as a kite on pink fairy dust and caffeine. But it seems to be a bit too tricky for our political masters, who should be taking seriously meaningful steps towards promoting sustainable agriculture before the crisis arrives. But they're not doing it. Perhaps all they can see, in their short-sighted politicians' way, is Cheap Food For the Masses: a policy it would be political suicide to tinker with. (That's 'suicide for them', of course, as opposed to 'suicide for all of us' as a result of their short-sightedness and cowardice.)

I guess all this will explain, if you haven't already worked it out for yourself, which I'm sure you will have... why the tomatoes you buy in *Crappo's* taste of... *noth*ing. They *look* like tomatoes, if rather anaemic ones; they *feel* right, except that you can't dent them with your thumb, or your nail come to that; they even slice right, sort of... but why do they taste only of slime? It's because British producers have been screwed by *Crappo* to produce the 'best' product at the lowest price: 'best', meaning of course, 'cheapest-while-*looking*-like-the-real-thing': or in other words: 'the cheapest, most deceptive crap we can get away with'. And anyway, most of *Crappo's* toms are grown hundreds of miles away, in Spain, or even further afield, and trundled up to us while still unripe, so they can slowly 'ripen' twixt truck and shelf. But they never do *ripen*, do they? The reason French toms in France taste richly of tomato is that they are grown to proper ripeness by local farmers for local consumption by people who actually care what their food tastes like and does to them. They've not been brainwashed by monopolist advertising, as we have.

The top reason why you should not only grow your own food as much as you can, but should also grow it as organically as you can, is that only organic systems care for the soil as a living entity, and thus ensure the sustainability of farming and the human race.

Non-organic systems will inevitably lead to destruction of the world's soil. And with no soil, there can be no plant life; no plant life means no animal life; no animal life means Good Night One and All. No point in asking the last person to leave the planet to please turn the lights off. They'll have gone off long ago.

So, the answer to the question **'Why Organic?'** is:

'For the sake of the health of everyone, from the microlife in the soil we all depend on, to our own children, ourselves, and future generations'.

Where do you do it?

Just about anywhere that has access to light and water.

If you have your own garden, you will be amazed at how much food you can grow in it if you go about it in a thoughtful manner. All will be revealed...

But what if you haven't got a garden or only a titchy one? Well, it's time to get ingenious... the way any organic gardener should.

Obviously, you can start by applying for a Council allotment. There's a national waiting list of 100,000 as I write, and you'll be at the bottom of your local one. But don't be downhearted. If you are determined, you can bring about rapid change. It's up to you... and a couple of mates, perhaps? The more the merrier (see Chapter 19 for a few tips).

Within a mile of your house or flat there will be at least one garden that has gone to rack and ruin for a number of reasons. If you can't actually see any such garden, ask around. Someone will know of one. Maybe the owner has got too old to manage it. If so, they would quite likely be happy for you to take over the running of it, in exchange for a few of the veg you grow.

Maybe there's a park nearby. Maybe the Council would be amenable to helping you set up an educational gardening patch in one corner. You don't have to be an expert to do this. An awful lot of kids have never seen a proper vegetable plant, never mind a seed. Anything you can produce will be a wonder to them, and after a couple of seasons you really will know what you're doing, and be helping and encouraging the kids to take part and perhaps to even find other plots for themselves, to earn a bit of pocket money, maybe. It's a very wise idea to get the kids on your side anyway, especially the older ones, *especially* if they look shifty and wear their silly hats backwards. Get a couple of 'leaders' to lend a hand and you'll never have any trouble with vandalism.

You might try the same idea at a local school or rugby club or cricket club or church/temple/mosque. Engage parents' support wherever possible.

Thinking a little further afield: who supplies your local greengrocer (if you still have one) or health food shop with organic veg? Ask. Look in the phone book for anyone who looks like he might be an organic farmer or grower. If he's within cycling range, pedal out to see him one day. Tell him you're interested in organics but have no experience and can't find an allotment anyway. Give him a moment to think. He might just offer to let you grow a bit of stuff on a corner of his place. If not, ask him if you could come out once a week, say, and learn about growing by helping him out on his land. Unless he's a real jerk, and very few organic people are, he will welcome a bit of help with open arms. Once he has seen how willing you are, and how tidy and reliable, and all those other things, I'll put a 50p bet on him offering you a small patch of your own the following season. If he doesn't... ask. Offer to pay a modest rent. Assure him you'll keep it tidy and that you'll be growing stuff mainly for your family, and will definitely be buying your bulk requirements, like spuds and mangel wurzels from him. And point out that over the course of the past year you have brought him six new customers for his 'veg box' service. (A veg box service is a home delivery service that many organic growers have adopted. You place an order, week by week, and they will supply whatever they can. Some will supply only what's in season, meaning what they have grown themselves; others will buy in organic oranges and so on to cover a broader spectrum.)

After your first season of growing, suggest that you could handle a little more land, if that's alright. Explain why. If he thinks you're up to it, he'll almost certainly be happy with this, if only for a bit of company more often. Farming these days is a lonely business. Machines are not great conversationalists.

Maybe if you have a trailer on your bike you'll already be helping him out with the odd light box delivery, on your way home, sort of thing.

You can see where this is leading, can't you?

It is entirely possible that within a couple of years, this farmer or grower might welcome the idea of opening up a little more of his land to allotmenteers, with you in charge of it, to make sure organic standards are kept to (more on organic standards in Chapter 19). This organic requirement will keep out all the people you don't want, and bring in all the ones you do want. And, of course, you can collectively make a big thing about it in the local press, and encourage schools to visit and for you to visit schools. Education, education, education...

Sooner or later you will be working co-operatively with the farmer on many levels, to the great benefit of all.

The organic world is a small one at the moment, and your farmer friend will be sure to talk to other farmers if he sees positive things coming out of his venture into allotments. Maybe a couple of these friends will try it themselves next year?

And, of course, if your own local farmer is a bit too far to cycle to, go in your car. But do go. With any luck you'll soon be taking three passengers with you, tools and all.

So there you are... by going and asking, and doing a tidy job, you could end up by starting a national trend: allotments for all again, but this time on farmers' land.

So... the answer to '**Where do you do it?**' is:

'Wherever you can find an ally if your own garden is a bit small'.

But be assured, you can grow a remarkable amount in a small space. We'll come to that in Chapter 6.

*Except the 'pink fairy dust', which is a total fabrication. (But give them time....)

**Tankers carrying milk pass each other, going in opposite directions, on the Franco-German border. Only an economist would try to explain this as rational behaviour.

Chapter 2
The Principles of Gardening

This will be a short chapter so pay attention or you'll miss it. Oh... and fetch an apple.

Ready?
Now eat the apple, but keep the core.

Gardening is so *simple*... just remember the fact that a seed has only one ambition in the whole world: it just wants to grow. That is what it is programmed to do by the mysteries of Nature. All a good gardener does is to enable the seed to do its thing. A bad gardener just gets in the way.

Now break open the apple core. Well, when you're ready then... Now... or any minute now... you will be holding an apple seed in the palm of your hand... NOW you are ready to receive the *Great and Mysterious First Principle of Gardening: **The Method**...* Are you ready?? (*Drum roll*) Are you sure?
Then here it is: the secret of gardening...

APPLY SEED A TO SOIL B
... and stand well back...

So simple.
Obviously it's not *quite* that easy, but if you remember you are just a facilitator, and let the seed do the work, you won't go far wrong.

First of all, try and think like a seed. No... go on... try it. Pick a seed from the core (perhaps you'd better cut the core open to save time...) and roll it in your hand. Look closely at it. Stroke it. It is absolutely amazing, is it not, that that insignificant apple pip, if you just help it a little by planting it, will one day grow into a full sized apple tree, maybe twenty feet tall, bursting into thousands of pink and white blossoms in the spring, every spring, and maturing into hundreds of marvellous edible fruits in the autumn, every autumn, for twenty years or more? And every single one of these fruits will contain half a dozen near perfect copies of that seed you are holding in your hand at this moment: perhaps thirty or fifty thousand in all... and all from that single seed nestling in your palm. Better still... no two of these seeds will be absolutely genetically identical. If you were to plant them all, you would get tens of thousands of trees each bearing slightly different apples. That seed in your palm might well be the grandparent of *The Best Apple in the World, Ever!* if you were to put the time and effort into all the propagation and selection.

Let your sense of wonder free for a few more moments... Just an apple pip; placed into the soil; moisture... it will send down a little root, then send up a pair of leaves. Then, as the light works its magic, photosynthesis will take over, and assuming the cat doesn't dig it up out of spite (cats, eh?) within a few months it will have produced a wide circle of roots, a stem, twigs, leaves... and all from what? The seed? But there weren't any roots or leaves in that seed, were there? So where did they come from... let your sense of wonder free again for a few moments. We are dealing with profound mysteries here. They may be everyday and 'common or garden'... but they are still profound mysteries.

Feel the seed again, and think 'What do you want, little life? How can I help you?' Try not to feel silly doing this. Anything creative starts with empathy.

So... without having so far read a single practical thing about 'gardening', where do you think your apple seed would like to be planted? Broadly speaking...? Spend a few moments on this... maybe shut your eyes... 'How can I help you?'

***

Welcome back.

I'm quite certain that you, a total beginner, will have come up with something like...

"I think this seed would like to be planted somewhere not too wet and not too dry; into soil with some nourishment in it; where there's plenty of light and air and not too many cats; not too close to the house, because it will grow big; not too close to anything else at all, really; it should be easy to reach to pick the fruit eventually, and to prune if I want to. And how deep should I plant the seed? Well, obviously, it's only a little seed so it can't go very deep, can it, or it would run out of energy before it reached the surface... About half an inch to an inch? Maybe it would like a little water to get it started?"

And you would be absolutely spot on in every respect.
So, like I said.. gardening is *easy*.

Would you like to try a carrot next? If you don't have a seed to hand, imagine a scruffy scaly looking item a couple of millimetres long. You can just about pick it off your palm with thumb and forefinger, but I warn you it's likely to get stuck under your fingernail. Got it? Good...
Right... using your skill and wisdom from your apple planting experience above... How would you go about growing a carrot? I'll leave you to it for a few moments...

***

Welcome back again.
A bit trickier, this, as you probably don't have an actual seed to chat to, but I imagine you might think something like this:

"I think this seed would like to be planted somewhere not too wet and not too dry; into soil with some nourishment in it; where there's plenty of light and air and not too many cats; not too close to the house, because it won't get enough rain or light there; not too close to anything else at all, really, as it needs its own space... perhaps a few inches either way? How deep should I plant the seed? Well, obviously, it's only a little seed so it can't go very deep, can it, or it would run out of energy before it reached the surface... About half an inch? Maybe it would like a little water to get it started?"
Spot on, again.
You will have noticed that the little passage above is remarkably similar to your ideas for planting a whopping great apple tree. Why is that, do you think? Yes, it's because what

matters for all seeds is pretty much the same stuff, namely:

1   Air, light, moisture, and nourishment
2   Thoughtful consideration for its elbow space
3   Sowing according to the size of the seed

In fact, if you can get the nourishment in the soil right up, it is remarkable how closely you can plant some crops. You can grow a decent carrot in a space smaller than a beer mat. More details shortly.

The business about the cats is really symbolic of one of a gardener's constant problems. Another 1,2,3 coming up:

1   First you get the soil right
2   Then you sow the seeds right
3   Then comes the tricky bit: *keeping* the plants

Nature doesn't seem to think that just because you did all the work that you should keep all the spoils. Right from the word 'go' there will be critters of all sizes queuing up to share your crop with you. It has always been like that, and as far as I can see, it always will be. It is this problem that ultimately lies behind conventional chemical farmers using ever more powerful poisons on their crops. And because of the way they go about their farming, they are largely correct in this. Organic farmers, however, do not use powerful poisons because they do their farming differently.

As an organic gardener you will need to be as thoughtful and vigilant as an organic farmer. Your aim is to prevent disease and pests rather than dealing with them when they arrive. Sometimes you can't prevent them, of course, and then you need to think even harder. More on this later, but for the moment let's consider the two commonest garden pests: the common child (*Brattus vulgaris*) and the pet (*Felix crappans* and *Canis excavatorans*).

All three of these nuisances can be controlled with forethought. The Child can be inducted into the whole gardening process, and be given a tiny patch behind the rhubarb, from where radishes can be eaten straight from the mud. The Dog will usually respond to the Big Finger and NO! Naughty! A bit of a barrier will help too. It will concentrate the mind. Think 'Homer Simpson'. The Cat is a different matter, particularly *Felix immigrans*, which may turn up from half a mile away to poo in your lettuces. The best answer to this problem, I think, is probably to resign yourself to a vigil or two, armed with a high-powered water-pistol full of very stale, very old urine. Add pepper or chilli powder to taste. Well, not literally, obviously.

***

A final thing, especially if you have a child: line a jam jar or similar with a layer or two of absorbent paper; kitchen towel perhaps. Can you still buy blotting paper? That's perfect. Add a half inch of water and let the paper get good and moist. Then slip a dry bean or two between the glass and the paper and put the jar on a windowsill where it will get as much light as possible. Make sure the paper never dries out. Within a couple of days you will see the bean swell... and then the magic begins. If you've never done this before, prepare to be amazed. I won't spoil it for you. Just do it, and watch your child's face, day by day...

You can use any sort of bean, or any seed at all, really. A big runner bean makes a wonderful display. You might like to soak it for a couple of hours before sliding it down the jar, but it probably doesn't need it.

Chapter 3
The Organic Technique

No doubt you are already pretty committed to the organic approach to gardening or you wouldn't have bought this book, but just to reassure you that it's not all a matter of sustaining the quality of the soil (which it is, above all else) and supplying healthy nutritious food for your kids (which it is), but also about that most immediate of sensations in a food: taste!

May I suggest that you buy a half kilo of chemical carrots and ditto organic carrots, and do a blind taste test on your kids (and neighbours, if it comes to that). I would be amazed if a single person couldn't taste the difference. I've offered samples of my organic carrots to many ladies of a certain age, and without exception they've looked wide-eyed, and said 'Ooo... I'd forgotten that carrots ought to taste like this.' This is because the entire country has been brainwashed over the last fifty years by the various *Crappo Incs* into accepting pallid orange skittles that taste faintly of soap as being what carrots 'are like'.

Try the same with a couple of tomatoes.

Of course, it isn't all down to the chemical or organic regime. Variety comes into it too. It is generally not known that supermarket tomatoes, for example, are selected not for nutritional value or taste, but for long shelf-life (more profit) and thick skins (less bruising in transit = more profit); and, of course, identikit shapes (supermarkets have brainwashed people into thinking *identical* tomatoes are *good* tomatoes). Now people only 'want' identikit tomatoes, even if they do taste only of sour slime (long term slick marketing and packaging = enormous profit).

Carrots and tomatoes are the two crops you will taste the difference most readily in, but potatoes are up there too, and onions. Anyway, you will no doubt make your own mind up about these things as you go.

So... now let's get stuck into *The Organic Technique:* it's very simple, as is gardening. It's only when you mess with chemicals, or try to force things unnaturally that it gets complicated.

The essence of the Organic Technique in a nutshell: or rather two nutshells:

1   **Feed the Soil:** Because *Crappo Inc* is squeezing *them* so hard, chemical farmers are desperate to squeeze every last penny of profit out of the land. Marginal land is ploughed up; unsuitable land is plastered with herbicides and fertilisers; what was once wildlife habitat, and hedgerows by the mile, are grubbed out to squeeze another ton of corn or cabbages from the soil, and to hell with tomorrow. The farmers know perfectly well that they are slowly wrecking their soil structure, but what can they do? Soon the soil will be reduced to humus-free dust and will dry out and crack, then flood... because it will no longer support the earthworms which are vital to soil life and structure. Bad farming in the USA produced the infamous dust bowls and the miseries depicted in *The Grapes of Wrath*. Ill-treated soil will not last forever...

Working *with* Nature, rather than trying to batter it into submission, involves looking very carefully at the land. No two fields are identical; no two allotments; not even any two square metres of garden. Try going to a local park or riverbank; or walk slowly round your own garden, or peer into a neighbour's. Look very carefully at what is growing in one place and not in another. Some patches are damper. Some have lots of ants. Some have patches of nettles. Some are just bare; others lush. Buttercups here, but not over there. See if you can work out what this all means, if you wish, but the real point of the exercise is to learn to see the land not just as Stuff, but an immensely complex and varied meld of rock dust and pebbles, trillions of microscopic living creatures, billions of larger critters like beetles and bugs, millions of worms and centipedes, decaying vegetable matter, moisture, and, though it may not be obvious, air and light. Every square foot is different.

Obviously, as a gardener, you don't want to be planting one carrot seed here and two more over there. You need a certain degree of homogeneity. That's fine. The smart thing is to not just plaster everywhere with your compost, but to concentrate the right input in the right place. More on this later. Modern chemical farmers now have satellite-controlled computer systems in their bus-sized tractors which will enable them to add a little extra fertiliser to this tiny bit and not that one. This is some sort of progress, maybe?

Meanwhile, you and I can cut out the satellite by walking and thinking.

2   **Compost and Recycle:** In observing how Nature does it, we see that nothing is ever wasted. Every single biological scrap is eventually recycled. It moves from one body to another, often via an amazingly complex chain of digestive systems. An oak leaf is pulled into the earth by a worm and is then broken down by an enormous army of small creatures, releasing the nourishing molecules as they go, ready for re-absorption by another plant.

It is this observed process of 100% recycling that led a couple of bright people over the last hundred years or so to experiment with systematic composting. Obviously, peasants had been doing similar things for centuries. The Chinese were particularly skilled, even using human waste, and not killing everybody off in the process, as their present population problem is testament to. It can be done. (No, I do not recommend using human waste unless you know precisely what you are doing. Composting toilets are worth investigating in, of course, and I can foresee a time when we'll all be using them).

Every organic gardener *must* have a compost heap. You can buy all manner of fancy boxes and tubs. Buy one if you like. No doubt they work well if used properly. But I've always got excellent results from rough old boxes made from scrap. One 'model', made from four old sash windows, glass and all, with an old rubber gym mat on top, produced remarkably good compost.

What are the principles of composting?

• By accumulating organic (meaning here 'once alive') waste into a pile, we encourage biological action: 'rotting down'. The thoroughly rotted down material is called 'compost'.
• An ideal box is roughly a cubic metre in size. Smaller is fine. Much smaller is not so fine.
• The cubic metre is big enough to keep in most of the heat which will be generated by the biological action. Smaller boxes hold less heat.
• To keep more heat in, we need to insulate the box. Details in a minute. Don't panic; it's very easy.
• Rotting is an aerobic activity, like jogging, only more productive. So we need to make air available to the heap.
• Rotting also requires water, unlike a fine single malt. So we need to ensure that the heap doesn't get too dry... or too wet, either. Hence:
• The box needs a cover. Old carpet over a scrap pallet works well: it allows excess water to run off, but will let a little soak through. Very good.

There you have it. If you want to do things the proper organic way, you will rescue a couple of doors or pallets off builders' skips and lash them together any old how. We are not talking *Grand Designs* here. String... wire... rescued nails... If you would rather practise your carpentry, I'll leave you to it. Just bear one or two things in mind: you'll need a sloping (to let rain run off) and openable (so you can add banana skins and hamster poo) lid; a means of eventually dismantling the front so you can shovel all that wonderful nutriment out and into a barrow; and you'll need to insulate it.

Newspaper is wonderful for this job. If you're using old pallets or doors, staple a length of nylon bean mesh, or an old nylon net curtain along one entire side, leaving the top edge open. This will be the inside of your box. You could also stretch a couple of pairs of old tights to do the job, but do make sure they are empty first or you'll never hear the end of it. If you're smart, you'll have laid several layers of newspaper over the door before stapling the mesh stuff onto it. If you've neglected to do this, you'll now have the fun of stuffing paper in, one issue at a time. The net or mesh should be nylon so it doesn't degrade too quickly. The paper will degrade of course. That's fine: more compost. You will need to replace it now and then.

Keep an eye open for too much old lead paint on rescued doors. Best to scrape off as much as you can. But a little bit isn't likely to hurt anyone. If in doubt, burn and scrape.

And don't despair if you really can't insulate your box to space shuttle standards. Try it without. If it's in a sheltered spot, you'll probably be fine.

A couple of other points:

Getting air in can be awkward. Could you lay three or four runs of old bricks or blocks or copies of Wisden or something, from the back of the box to the front? Then lay something air-permeable on top? A bit of pallet? A layer of scrap pig mesh (of which, more in Chapter 9) or chicken mesh? Or a rough weave of shrubby prunings? Maybe, if you've got stiff enough prunings, you could do without the bricks? You get the point: anything to help a bit of air to get in from below. You might also shove a pole into the heap and waggle it about from time to time. But unless you've been adding too much heavy stuff at once, you shouldn't need to.

I've made excellent boxes from double layers of pig mesh stuffed with newspapers. But of course I live on a farm so I have odd bits of mesh to hand.

Would it be possible to use a boundary wall as one side of the heap? A house wall would even add a bit of extra warmth. This 'free wall' will save a bit of space and work. But be sure to insulate it if possible, unless it is a house wall (a couple of nails or pegs into the mortar to hold the nylon: stuff with newspaper as before, or use the cardboard box that your latest fridge came in. It will eventually rot, of course, but that's fine.).

In dry weather, use your washing up water in a watering can to keep the heap damp. Don't use ordinary detergent though. Get some suitable degradable stuff.

Believe it or not, compost heaps have been known to spontaneously catch fire. This is very unusual, and shows that someone wasn't keeping his eye on it. The heap should become hot or even very hot in normal use. If you get good at it you can control the heat so that even tough weed seeds are killed. Again, pay attention; keep watching; keep learning, just as you will from each plant and each yard of land. (The fire hazard is extremely low. I've never had a problem in thirty years.)

Every now and then you can turn and stir the mix with a fork if you fancy it. Personally, I wouldn't bother. Just scrape off the uncomposted stuff at the end of the process and use it in the next heap.

Now then: how to use this wonderful compost box...

Anything that was once alive counts as 'organic' in this context. Thus, all food scraps go in (not that you should have any scraps: leftovers should all go into soups or sandwiches, *as you well know*); hamster and rabbit litter; tea leaves (I'm sure you're not using ridiculously expensive and wasteful tea-*bags*... are you? Incidentally, some irresponsible oaf is now marketing *nylon* tea-bags. Would you believe it...?); lawn mowings; weeds; newspapers; cotton or woollen rags... You get the drift. If in doubt, leave it out. It's unlikely to actually harm the compost, but it can be a mess.

A little quiz:
Which of these items can go into a compost heap?

1   Egg shells
2   Old shoes
3   Oyster shells
4   Bones
5   Deceased rabbits
6   Corks
7   *The Sunday Times*
8   Old floorboards
9   Rotten fruit
10   All that caviar left over from Rachel's birthday
11   Food packaging
12   Rubber gloves and
13   ...er... 'you know whats'?
14   Cardboard boxes
15   Big balls of snot and paper hankies

16   Leaves
17   String
18   Dog poo
19   Feathers
20   Fat
21   Ash
22   Peach and plum stones
23   Hair trimmings
24   The contents of hoover bags
25   Romantic fiction.

1, 3, 9, 10, 15, 16, 18, 19, 23 and 24 are pretty well immediately 'yes'. But not too much at once, and bash the shell up a bit, and either dampen any dust, or sandwich it between layer of grass cuttings or something else squishy.

Everything else is 'it all depends....'

Except for 8, which is 'don't be silly'. Yes, wood is organic, but great big chunks... too much.

In a little more detail:

2:    Are you sure the shoes are leather? If so 'yes'. If not 'no'. Leather might take years to rot, but rot it eventually will.

4:    Bones are fine in theory but will they attract rats, badgers, polar bears, etc? Perhaps best to experiment a little.
Start with small bones, and bury them well inside the compost mass. Try beating bigger bones into bits then stirring them in.

5:    See 4. You may not wish to beat poor Flopsy to pieces, of course.

6:    If they *are* corks, good. Or are they plastic?

7:    See 8! Huge wads of paper are just too much. A bit at a time, preferably crunkled up to let some air in.

11:    Mmm... is it papier maché? Or more wretched plastic?

12:    Latex rubber or some sort of oil derivative? Oil derivatives don't count as organic. They really are chemicals, let's face it.

13:     Oh, for Pete's sake...

14:     See 7. Big thick stuff... no. Torn up and well dampened... yes. But not too much at once.

17:     If it's hairy sisal or white proper string, yes. If it's plastic of some sort, obviously no.

18:     But not too much at once, and bury it in the middle.

20:     See 4. Better to use the fat for birds or chop it into pets' food. Again, common sense all round...

21:     Wood ash yes, in moderation at any one time; coal ash no.

22:     Any sort of fruit stone is fine, but they will take time to break down. Crack them first?

25:     See 7. No matter how apparently steamy, 'romfic' is actually very stodgy stuff to a lively compost heap.

I guess you'll get the drift. Don't use too much of any one thing at any one time. A rich mix is best. Keep additions moist.

Lawn mowings can become a slimy problem if there's too much at once. Mix them in with some crinkled papers and hunks of cardboard.

Make friends with a greengrocer if you can; or maybe a veg packhouse on an industrial estate; or a restaurant owner; or (gasp!) a supermarket manager, and see if you can collect rubbish veg off them for your compost heap. You'll find *someone*.

Now for the personal challenge: compost needs two basic types of input: cellulose and nitrate. Anything remotely fibrous and woody counts as cellulose: in other words, plant refuse. The nitrate is harder to find as it's mainly sourced from animals. Rabbit sweepings or chicken litter are ideal. So is a few inches of horse muck if you can get it. Stables are only too glad to get rid of the stuff. Hire a truck if you must. A couple of tons of horse muck will give an allotment a couple of years of top fertility once it's rotted down. Ten tons is much better. Scatter a layer (raw is fine) on the compost heap after every few inches of other stuff.

If you're a bit pushed for horse muck, go for Vitamin P. This is a by-product of human digestion and comes in convenient liquid form. Store it in a tightly screwed tub until needed. Gentlemen often find it easier to collect than ladies, it should be said. To use, dilute roughly 50:50 with water and sprinkle on. Or just deliver direct, taking care not to miss the corners. If holding a barbecue, I leave the options up to you.

You can tell when the compost is 'done' by scraping back the surface and delving into the mass. If it's brown, rich and crumbly, it's perfect. If it's a bit sticky, it's probably still OK. If it stinks, it isn't ready yet. Compost should smell delightful. Your nose knows.

Another good sign is a mass of bright red 'brandling' worms wriggling through the heap. They provide the final conditioning process for you. Heaven knows where they all come from, but they always turn up.

There will aways be a few odd lumps that haven't broken down. Just sieve them out and chuck them into your next heap. Eventually they will rot.

Compost is the all-purpose fertiliser of choice. Just keep it coming. It really is worth hunting down some stables, or even a chicken factory, if you can stomach it. The chicken manure may not be strictly 'organic' as it may contain medicines and hormones, but it'll compost well enough, and will almost certainly break down all the residues in the process, especially if the heap heats up properly. Ask the owner about any chemicals that might be in the droppings and check on the internet for how likely the residue is to linger malevolently. Be cautious. No, I don't know of a suitable site, offhand. Do I have to do everything? Heavens...

If you don't have the space for a proper compost box, it's worth knowing that some councils subsidise specially designed composting tubs and boxes of various sorts. The kids might enjoy looking after a 'worm bin' for producing both worms and compost from cooked food and veg scraps. Buy them a book on it for Christmas... *Composting with Worms* by George Pilkington or Mike Woolnough's *Worms and Wormeries*.

***

The other three sorts of additives you might like to consider are leaf mould, lime, and rock dust.

Soil is basically *mineral* rock dust mixed with varying amounts of *biological* matter. One normally thinks of there being three sorts of soil: sand, clay, and loam. Sandy soil is, as you might imagine, very dry and loose, and won't hold moisture.

Clay is very stiff and a swine to dig, and won't let air or moisture in.

Loam... ah loam!... is what you want. Loam is either of the other two, or a mixture, with lots and lots of fragrant humus (rotted biological material, like compost) in it.

Very few soils are purely one or the other... A 100% sand 'soil' would be a beach, wouldn't it? We're talking 'preponderance' here.

A quick test for what your own soil is, is to pick up a moist handful and gently squeeze it, then open your palm. If it falls apart immediately when you poke it, then it's sandy; if it won't fall apart at all, it's clay. If, however, it crumbles gently, it's loam. You can get the same information just by looking, actually: rich, brown, crumbly... good enough to eat.. that's loam.

If you haven't got loam to start with, the next best thing is clay. It may be impossible to work, but there is at least something in it to bring out if you can get some organic matter into it. Sand is... nothing, and best used for digging into a clay patch to break it up a bit.

If your 'soil' is simply very sandy fullstop, then your priority must be to get some more 'body' into it. Clay will help. It will be the very devil to shift and spread, but it *will* help. Compost and muck will be invaluable, of course. Work + time = success. T'was ever so. No soil is hopeless.

It's perhaps worth mentioning that if your garden is a small workaday Victorian patch with a bit of a lawn and a few manky 'ornamentals', it's possible that the poor soil will have never been properly fed in its life. And that what little vivacity there was in it originally will by now have been all but exhausted. I've seen such soil which seems to be little more than grey dust. Even the weeds look ill.

The organic gardener's target is to convert his patch of rubble and junk into a deep bed of wonderful loam. Hence, you need to import as much organic stuff as you can. But it's no good in its raw state. It needs to be composted.

Leaf mould: Autumn leaves are very useful. Sweep them up wherever you can find them. Beat the Council to it. If a neighbour is planning a bonfire, offer to take all his leaves off his hands. But instead of composting them, pile them up somewhere, in a meshed-off corner perhaps, or stuffed tightly into old onion nets (donated by a greengrocer or your local mini-mart) and leave them to weather for a year or two. They will slowly break down to leaf mould. This has no real nourishment value, but it is very good as a soil conditioner, for busting up clay or bulking up sand, for example.

Lime: 'Lime' means 'calcium' to a gardener, and it is the prime means of reducing the acidity of soil. You can buy fancy pH kits (acidity is measured as 'pH': '0' means flesh-eating acid; '7' means neutral; '14' means flesh-eating alkali. You don't need to know this.) but most soils will grow most things, if properly maintained. It's as with people: eat proper food and you don't need extra vitamins and all the rest of that stuff in fancy jars and over-priced tubs.

Rock dust: Science has come to realise that a healthy person needs not just the major food groups of carbohydrate, fats and protein, but a welter of other items in tiny quantities. Some of these are called 'trace elements', and are taken up into plants from the minerals in the soil: things like selenium, phosphorus, zinc, copper...

Over the centuries, rich soils can use up all their trace elements, or have them washed out by rainfall, so people have been experimenting with replacing them with selected rock dusts scattered over the land. Some people claim remarkable results by doing this. I don't recommend rushing out and buying twenty tons, but you might like to look into it on the internet, particularly if your garden is a old neglected one. There's also an excellent book called *We Want Real Food* by *Archers* editor Graham Harvey which looks at rock dusting.

We're almost finished. Told you it was easy. There's a bit more on 'soil' in Chapter 5, but that's about it.

All I'd like to add here is that an organic gardener has very different aims from a commercial grower. Whereas a grower might have a contract to supply 2,000 cabbages a week, a gardener wants one plant a week or maybe two if his pet rabbits are getting frisky. Growers and farmers use what is called 'F1' seed. As you might imagine, F1 seeds are pretty fast growers, but more to the point, you can set your watch by them. Tuesday? Zooooooom... up they come: *all* of them. And twenty weeks later, or whatever, they are *all* ready for harvest. There is more to it than this, of course, but on balance, an ordinary gardener doesn't have much use for F1 seed.

What you want above all are varieties that will crop over a period, which are moderately pest resistant, which crop at a rate that suits you, and which are nutritious and delicious. More later.

***

I guess it goes without saying that an organic grower will be eating food according to a timescale that is quite different from the one *Crappo Omnium* encourages. Supermarkets go to enormous lengths to supply what they consider to be top quality everything, on every day of the year. Tomatoes from Africa, apples from New Zealand, peaches from Brazil... Whatever, from wherever.

Of course, it makes sense to have some international trading, especially of things we really can't grow here, like bananas and oranges, but this obsession with having absolutely everything available '24/7/52' needs to be reconsidered, I would suggest. As an example, what do you think about having out-of-season French beans *flown* in from Kenya? Or tiny immature sweetcorn flown halfway round the world from Thailand? Do we need these things? At the cost in fuel and pollution they bring? Do you buy such things? Do you think you ought to?

This must be a personal business, I think. Everyone must make their own choices. Personally, I don't object to importing apples from New Zealand, to get us through the summer, as apples are an important source of vitamins, but I won't buy out-of-season 'luxury' strawberries from China or Jupiter. You may consider me a hypocrite here. As I say, everyone should consider the issue and draw their own line for well-thought-out reasons.

Another good reason for not eating out-of-season strawberries is that they are utterly tasteless, are they not? They look like strawberries, but they have been bred for long shelf life and appearance, not for flavour or nutrition.

So, an organically inclined person will think carefully before buying veg out of season. Most people, however, have no idea what 'out-of-season' means any more. Commerce and advertising have persuaded us all (almost all) that 24/7/52 is what it's all about.

'So what's with the hair shirt?', you may be asking.

Apart from the huge amount of pollution and waste generated by endless and pointless transportation of too much of everything, it's to do with quality and treats, rather than quantity and routine. Grow your own spuds and you'll never be disappointed by watery tasteless things from Israel and Egypt again. Yours will be *resonant* with flavour. Your own carrots will taste rich and wonderful. When the earlies are gone, you move on to the maincrop. Then you look forward to the next earlies. Who's losing anything here? Not me. I suggest the losers are the poor souls who have been brainwashed into thinking that more equals better, and who think that if it looks like a strawberry, then the sticky and faintly medicinal taste is what it ought to be, 24/7/52. That's it. Piece of cake.

Speaking of which...

Chapter 4
Appropriate Fun

It's always been a rule of thumb for me that if you're enjoying it, it can't be work. And what makes organic gardening such fun is that you engage your whole being with it. You're not just a biological fitter, you are an active and creative force in the world. You choose your seeds and plants carefully, according to your circumstance and your own plot. You pay full attention to every one of your acts: what does the soil look like in this corner? What weeds are growing here? Isn't that little daisy a tiny miracle? Is that a robin? Oh... woodlice... Do we like woodlice? (No, not really. They don't cause much actual harm, but they show that something's a bit too dry.) Ah! A big beetle with a violet go-faster stripe down the side! Do we like beetles? (Yes we do. Beetles are good for the garden. They hunt down pests.)

You experiment constantly with new varieties and spacings and timings, and you use your ingenuity in ways you never have before. Oh wow! A friend has just given me sixteen toilet roll middles! Fantastic! Just what I wanted! (I'll leave you to work on that one.) Better still.. Almost five square yards of vinyl left over from someone's new kitchen floor! (Ditto.) Oh dear... our trusty old telly has finally expired in a roiling cumulus of green smoke. Excellent news... This means we can... (ditto...)

***

Probably the best thing you can bring to a garden is The Good Vibe. The brighter and happier you are, the better will your garden respond. If you don't believe me, it doesn't matter. Try it.

If you're in a bad mood, wait till you're feeling a bit brighter before you go outside. Once you're on the up, the garden will do the rest for you. Before long you'll be wondering what headache pills are for. It's all part of the organic principle of working *with* Nature and not *against* her. Co-operation is always better than domination, as any occupying army knows. Compare the mutual respect of indigenous peoples towards their forest with the modern consumerist mode of mass destruction of entire jungles for short-term profit. Who will win that exchange in the long run? And who will be impoverished by it?

***

As part of your creative engagement with your plot, you will be constantly thinking of ways you can achieve what you want without driving five miles to a huge garden centre and five miles back again. For thousands of years people somehow managed without garden centres. How did they do that, do you think? Well, obviously, they realised that all you *need* for a productive veg plot is seeds, a plot, and a couple of basic tools. You certainly don't need battery-powered carrot lifters and a crop-line delineator with six-jewel bearings and two titanium pegs with inbuilt laser for *Super Space-Age Accuracy!* All you need is a ball of string (bits knotted together work just fine) and two sticks. To sharpen the sticks a bit you will need to fly in the face of the law and buy a sheath knife: a good strong whittler. Good luck in finding one. If you can't, no doubt you can find something similar: every town has a *Psycho Shop* full of deliberately wicked-looking knives which are illegal to carry, and camouflaged Spandex thongs to go with your replica AK47.

So...
Tool 1: A good strong knife. Useful for all sorts of things, including, perhaps surprisingly, weeding (see Chapter 11).

What other tools do you need? Only basic stuff. All bar one will be buyable at boot sales:

Tool 2: A spade. These come in various sizes. My grandad had one with a blade the size of his trilby. Personally, I don't see the point of popping all your vertebrae by wielding a brute like that. I recommend a 'border spade' or 'ladies' spade'. Whatever it's called, it's got a blade the size of a standard hardback. You can dig just as much and just as quickly as with the huge Man Spade but without personal injury. And you can actually build up an enjoyable rhythm with it. 'Place; in; tip; lift; dump; place; in; tip; lift...' The big spade just exhausts you. 'Place; in...in... IN... oh bloody hell, *IN, you bastard...*'

Tool 3: A fork. As for the spade. You don't need a huge thing. Smaller is better, not least because you won't find yourself applying far too much leverage to the handle, thus snapping or bending it. It will do everything you need, just at the rate of a little less per lift.

A general point here: handles? Wood, plastic, or metal? There's probably not much to choose as long as you don't strain it. Personally, I'd steer clear of plastic. Everything plastic seems to rot and snap sooner or later. Wood, well oiled, seems to last forever. Metal too.

Wood is easiest to come by. Clean it (and the blade) down with the back edge of your sheath knife, wipe over with the traditional filthy rag; then a clean rag; then rub it good and hard with a couple of coats of oil. What sort of oil?

Crappo Garden Mega-Centre NanoLubricol Tool Handle Gel,
now with added crapolase enzymes for a softer skin

No... chip oil. Second-hand is fine. What a wonderful aroma to accompany your spring digging. Keep a bottle of old chip oil handy for all garden tool cleaning jobs.

Think carefully before digging with a spade. Would a fork be OK? A spade is good for chopping through hard soil, and for inverting the weeds so they can rot; a fork is much quicker and takes less energy. Very good for softer land with just a few weeds to be shaken clean and dumped in the compost heap. As always, pay attention, do nothing 'on automatic', and experiment.

Tool 4: A rake. These come in all sizes. You may like to buy a one-foot-wide one and a two-foot-wide one (for a pittance at boot sales). The smaller one will be useful for fine work, like preparing a seed bed; the larger one will be good for general hacking, hauling and battering. My favourite rake is of middling size, and has a steel handle. It's good for all soil work, and for heaving brambles onto a bonfire too. Also for threatening cats with.

Tool 5: A hoe. There are dozens of types of hoe. I suggest you only need one type, and it is *not* the traditional one with a D-shaped blade (often called a Dutch hoe). What you most need a hoe to do is kill weeds. The stabbing motion of a D hoe is exhausting and almost completely pointless. Think about it...

What you really want is a tool that slides along, parallel with the surface of the soil, which slices the top of the weed from its root. Is there such a tool? Yes! There are several new models which work like this. The one I've used a lot and recommend wholeheartedly is the *Wilkinson Swoe*. It looks a bit like a demented golf club, and has a fine steel blade, sharpened on three sides, which slices through weeds like a knife through hot butter. You can cut on the pull and the push, and on the sideways swipe, as if wedging your way out of a tricky bunker. You can hoe all the way round a three-foot-wide courgette plant from one spot. It has an aluminium handle, so it's very light and won't rust. You won't get much change out of £20-25, but it's worth every penny. I know from experience that you can hoe a long path between beds of veg clear of small weeds at a slow walking pace.

Tool 6: A trowel. There are lots of pretty-looking trowels around. Don't be fooled. You want something that is built to work hard and to last. Pressed steel is useless. Boot sales are good: look for a really solid blade, really solidly attached to, guess what? A really solid handle. 'Solid' is a key word here. And I wouldn't bother at all with those tiny little 'weeding forks' that look so neat in a set with a rubbishy 'trowel'. I was given one thirty years ago and have never used it once. More on weeding tools in Chapter 16.

That's about it. I guess a few other items will eventually clutter up your shed/porch/kitchen, but I advise resisting them until you are certain you'll get use out of them. A shed, of course, is ideal for sitting in when it's raining. Much better than a kitchen. A few of those three gallon black plastic buckets you sometimes find in £1 shops are handy. So is a wheelbarrow. DON'T get a plastic one. A pneumatic tyre is usually worth the extra. It's remarkable how much easier pneumatic-shod wheels are to push over anything other than a billiard table. Speaking of which, if your shed is big enough, a billiard table is a sound investment.

Or at least a pool table. Cover it with a slab of fibreboard, staple a length of old vinyl over it and, voilà... a perfect solid working surface, easily demountable for an evening of low-budget fun. If you're feeling flush, why not fix the worktop to a few cords and pulleys, and screw a couple of gaily coloured light bulbs to the under surface, and haul it up to the rafters at the end of a busy day. Flick on the stereo... and you have your own speakeasy. Easy, if rather silly.

You really can get by very well indeed with just a few tools, but your own plot will eventually tell you what else you need. For example, a clayey patch might call for a 'cultivator', which is like a three-clawed hacking rake. Sandy soil might want a 'draw hoe' from time to time. This is a variation on the sort of tool they seem to use all over Africa. It has a small blade, at right angles to the handle. Good for 'drawing' soil towards you; but usually a rake will do this well enough.

That's about it for bought-in tools. You may enjoy making others, of course. When we were growing veg commercially, I designed and made a couple of 'multi-dibbers' from odd bits of scrap plywood, and pegs cut from poles from the hedgerow. These pegs were of various interchangeable lengths. Some were two inches long and others just a half inch or so. The idea was that you laid the dibber along the row line (ie, the marker string) and jumped on it. This would leave a dozen or so indentations in the soil, just deep enough to drop, say, parsnip seed into, or an onion 'set' (of which more later) depending upon the depth of the indentation or hole. You then pick up the dibber, and repeat the process a little further up. Using this tool I could mark out 1,200 'holes' in a row, again at a slow walking pace. The alternative, of using the traditional sharpened old spade handle to dib one hole at time, would have taken hours and driven me nuts.

I'm not suggesting that you will need such a tool, of course, but you may think of something else that you could make yourself that would reduce the donkey work for you.

A rotavator? No. Not unless you know what you're doing and why, and can't do the job better by hand. They do have their uses on large patches of land, but I could weed my crops more quickly and efficiently using hand tools than with our rotavator. And if you use them for primary cultivation, they also tend to 'pan' the soil immediately under the level where the rotary motion slices through the soil. Obviously, this happens most easily on clay soil, and can prove a real problem, as water will not be able to permeate the shiny (but invisible to you) surface.

Also, what you are trying to do is to develop a relationship with every inch of your plot. A noisy, smelly and cantankerous rotavator is not the best ally for this.

***

Invention and ingenuity... an organic plotter's best friends. Not just in saving lots of money, but for their own sakes. It's my opinion that the reason so many people are so dispirited and depressed in a Britain that has never been so wealthy, is not because they don't have enough money but because they have no creativity in their life. We have all been consumerised into thinking that *buying* a solution is the best way. Therefore what we *always* need if we have some sort of problem, is more money. *Crappo*! What cheers and enlivens people is creativity: either discovering creative solutions to problems or making the solutions themselves, preferably out of cardboard and yoghurt pots; or re-thinking the issue until you discover it's not a problem at all... merely a situation, that you might choose to deal with in a number of ways, or possibly even ignore completely. At best, you might learn to embrace it. It's all in the mind. Crisis? Or opportunity?

Right... How did you get on with the sixteen toilet roll middles? What ideas did you come up with? The immediate use that occurs to me is to stuff them with soil or potting compost, and plant a sweetcorn seed into each one. Keep them damp, cosied up on a seed tray, until the time is right (ah... timing!) and the plants look strong, then trowel sixteen holes of roughly the right size, fill them with water, then drop a loo roll into each one. Firm the soil back round them. The roots will grow out through the bottom of the tube and the thin cardboard will eventually rot down, although you might prefer to slit it or remove it before planting to give the roots immediate access to their food source. Collect some more for next year.

The vinyl? Again, the obvious use to me would be to use it as a weed suppressant. Any patch of land new to cultivation will probably be rich in heavy duty weeds like dock and nettles. You will eventually need to hack them out, but meanwhile you can just cover them over winter with something that keeps the light out. No light, no growth. Not quite true, as the roots contain enough energy to get the plant going (Remember the bean in the jar? A seed this time, not a root, but the principle is the same), but if it doesn't get light sooner or later, even the toughest weed will have to succumb. No doubt you can think of other uses for vinyl. I used off-cuts to make rainproof surfaces to the roofs of some bird boxes. It would also make good anti-clubroot collars (see Chapter 15).

The expired telly? Not obvious, this one, and maybe it won't apply at all if you have a modern flat-screen model. But we keep our herbs under control (especially mint, which will run up your trouser leg if you stand too close to it) by sinking a couple of 'telly-backs' into the bed, and filling them with soil. There's enough soil in the plastic 'back' for the plant to thrive, but the ventilation slits are not wide enough to let the major roots escape.

I'll add a couple more suggestions below, but meanwhile here's one to work your imagination on: empty plastic pop bottles. I can think of three uses off-hand. I bet you can beat that. Let's compare notes at the end of this chapter.

Old windows... very hard for builders to re-use it seems. But they make excellent cold frames. A cold frame is a sort of miniature greenhouse, just a foot or so high. A few bricks or blocks, topped with a window or two. Voilà...

Bubble wrap, if you can get to it before *Brattus vulgaris* has popped it all... also useful as a cold-frame cover. What's more, it has good insulating properties. Think 'plant protection'. If you can get a crop a week earlier than normal, well... good. And, of course, you can crop a week later, too, at the end of the season.

Old cassette or vhs tape... strung between twigs and poles can help to keep birds off crops. CDs flapping about can help too. I bet the entertainment industry never thought it could be so useful.

Those one-litre fruit juice containers... cut in half and pierced at the bottom... excellent plant pots, like the toilet roll middles. Except that these are re-useable.

Big cardboard trays from supermarkets... excellent seed trays. But be careful when lifting them, as they might like to fall apart amusingly after being carefully watered for several weeks. Experiment with a plastic bag lining... but make sure the whole tray can drain properly.

Old pill tubs or 35mm film tubs... just the job for dropping over the top of low plant stakes. There's nothing quite like a narrow bamboo pole straight up your nose for making your eyes water. Except one straight into your eye, of course. They are also convenient for carrying small seeds in when planting out. Paper packets can get claggy and crumpled. Plastic tubs don't. You might even become skilled enough to shake carrot seed accurately direct into the soil from a shiny plastic tub. Maybe an adapted old salt shaker would be even better? Or any old disposable plastic bottle with a nozzle that can be suitably reamed out to size?

Old electric leads and cables make good weatherproof ties

for supporting wobbly jobs like tomatoes to those bamboo poles above. The three pin plug makes a last resort down-on-your-knees scarifier/scrubber for the odd moments when no other sort of weeder or hoe will do the job. Also handy for grooming stubborn knots out of the coats of retrievers and grubby children's hair. No, perhaps not.

It's all about staying creatively alert. There's no such thing as rubbish: only resources. Yes, obviously, I'm exaggerating, but you see my point, I'm sure. Think twice about every single thing you are tempted to throw out. What *use* might you find for it in the garden?

How did you get on with the pop bottles challenge? My three ideas are:

Cut out the bottoms, unscrew the tops, and use as individual mini-greenhouses for developing seedings. Keep them in situ with weights or wire pegs.

Pierce the bottom, fill with soil ('How' I'll leave to you...), hack a few holes in the sides and plant a wild strawberry plant in each hole. Hang by the back door, out of reach of *Brattus v.* Substitute pansies, wild garlic (ransomes) or chives at will.

I've forgotten the third one...

No, wait a minute...

Cut off the bottom, remove the cap, and sink into the ground at an angle, near a big plant like a tomato. Use it as a funnel for watering into if we (ever) have a dry summer (again). A bit of water near the roots is better than a lot sprinkled all over and nowhere. This is particularly useful in a greenhouse or polytunnel. See Chapter 13 for a little more about greenhouses etc.

Just one final point: ignorant people 'think' that the organic method is some sort of backward step to medieval times, whatever that's supposed to mean, and that we poor deluded organic idiots enjoy nothing better than ploughing up an old pasture with our bare fingers. Don't bother with these people. Let the children play.

And don't respond when they notice that you've finally seen the light because they've caught you out using a flame weeder, or *plastic* to cover your new tunnel cloche.

Again: the whole point of the organic approach is to work with Nature as far as possible, using your attention, creativity and imagination, instead of blindly following someone else's rules. Once in a while, you may decide that hiring a rotavator, or indeed a JCB, is the most appropriate answer to a particular problem. And there is nothing wrong with plastic in itself. Use it wisely, for a creative purpose, and then re-use it as often as possible. There is no harm in this.

Chapter 5
More on Soil

Basically, an organic grower is concerned with the *soil*.
Treat the soil right, and your plants will grow healthy. They
can't avoid it. Eat healthy food, and you will grow healthy too.
Obviously this doesn't mean that you will never fall sick, but
you will be stronger than average when it comes to fighting
back.

Treating the soil means feeding it (with compost above all),
opening it up to light and water and air (by digging in leaf
mould, for example) and redressing any weaknesses by top
dressings of limestone or other rock dust. A key point is that
any dressing *must* be slow release. I guess you've passed a farm
somewhere with clouds of billowing white stuff everywhere.
That will be lime... in a very fine powdery form, for immediate
absorption (or immediate blowing away, of course). Organic
folk have longer targets. Slow release and gradual balancing
is what we want. We're aiming to build a soil that will last for
decades: sustainability. An unsustained soil will eventually
either wash away or blow away. And guess what...? They ain't

making land any more. Once it's gone, it's gone.

Sustainable soil in farming and growing is an *utterly* and desperately important matter.

***

People's bodies are made up of roughly 70% water; plants are much the same.

Water is a truly remarkable substance. Ask any physicist. All of life depends upon it. No water, no life.

Having said that, of course, someone is bound to write to tell me of some extremophile microbe somewhere that can only live in solid granite or boiling nitric acid. Thank you in advance for the information, and for your trouble. The only response I can possibly make is 'You call *that* living'? I think you'll get the point, whatever: Life as we know it, Jim... needs water.

Water comes into gardens and plots mainly directly from the sky. Rainwater is the best water for growing plants with, you will not be surprised to learn. It even contains traces of nourishing nitrate from all the lightning that has blasted through it.

Tap water, if extracted from rivers, often contains purifying chemicals and also many other stray chemicals (including traces of pesticide, herbicide and fungicide run-offs from chemical farms, and rather too many female hormones, courtesy of the contraceptive pill. A report published in 1999 by the UK Environmental Agency reported that 57% of the roach in one river have changed sex. I'll leave you to work that one out, and roughly what it might be doing to people.)

It thus makes sense for an organic grower to collect rainwater whenever possible. A big tub or barrel of some sort, plumbed into a handy downspout from the roof is the obvious solution. You can then either drain water into a couple of watering cans at back-wrenching floor level, before you hobble off à la *Sorcerer's Apprentice* to the gasping veg patch, or at a rather less agonising knee-level, if you put the barrel on a bit of a plinth. Either way, you then haul the cans twenty to fifty feet down the garden and sprinkle it on the grateful salads.

Alternatively... and being an organophile you will be very interested in anything alterative... you can do a bit of a calculation, and store your rainwater barrel on a plinth that will be a couple of feet higher than any point in your garden. You can see what's coming, can't you? Yes, you then attach a hose pipe to the barrel, and a tap to the end of the pipe. You then drag the pipe across the garden to wherever suits you. Several options are now available:

You can drain the water into the cans, as before, but more or less in situ. A great saving in effort here.

Or... you can haul the pipe around the garden, watering as you go. There are some really nice attachments to help with this, including a neat two-foot wand with adjustable spray head.

You might even possibly use the hose to deliver direct into upturned pop bottles next to large plants or the gooseberry bush (But not radish, obviously. Be sensible!). Or you might have installed a cunning system of gently sloping irrigation channels, made from fifty yards of old guttering you rescued from a skip. This guttering might have holes drilled out here and there to allow for delivery precisely where you want it.

Or... you can attach the first hose to a 'leaky hose' of some sort. You can buy this or make it. The bought sort is made of semi-permeable rubber which allows water to very slowly soak through it and into the soil near your plant roots. If you bury it by an inch or two you won't lose water to evaporation. Neat, eh? You can make your own from any sort of pipe that suits you. I guess you could drill out scrap steel pipes if they come for free. Personally, if you're going to bury it, I would stick to plastic hosepipe of some sort, as being less jarring on the spine when you've forgotten precisely where it is, and accidentally whack into it with a spade.

By trial and error you will know how big to make the holes, precisely where you want them, and how high to open the tap. A word of warning: this can be a bit of a business if your land slopes. I once had an experimental system made from very thin polythene tubing which I gaffer-taped to the feed pipe. I poked holes in with a tack and switched on. Naturally, and in accordance with several well-known Laws of Physics, the water refused to come out of the upper holes at all, but shot out like a Belgian fountain from all the lower ones, completely missing the plants, but alarming the chickens. I tried regulating the flow by crimping clothes pegs onto the tubing here and there. This did improve things, but it was never a great success, and I got wetter than I wanted to in the process. Incidentally, I think I discovered en route that the optimum spacing between the pegs would probably have been a logarithmic one. Something new every day.

If you're bothered that the static water in the barrel might attract mosquitoes or vampire bats, pour a few drops of old chip oil onto the surface. Vampires hate chips.

***

Chemical farmers tend to have trouble with the three water-borne pests of drought, flood and erosion if the weather is a bit over the top. Organic ones are rather less discomfited. Why?

Take 'drought': because the biological matter we organic types put into the soil holds water like a sponge, a dry period is not too much of a problem. But consider soil without organic matter. What do you have? Inorganic matter, meaning 'rock particles'. Do rock particles hold water? No. Sand lets it straight through. Clay keeps it on the surface.

Take 'flood': biological matter which supplies the nourishment to plants is less likely to be swept entirely away than highly soluble chemical fertilisers are. Already, fertiliser wash-off is a threat to our streams and wildlife. But not from organic farms it isn't.

And 'erosion': rock dust, soaked in soluble chemicals is clearly more vulnerable to aggressive wind and water than land packed with intricate networks of rootlets and biological detritus.

In a word: any farmer who neglects to return biological matter to his soil is slowly but surely killing it. Alright, that was seventeen words. Not to worry.

***

This might be as good a place as any to discuss planting and sowing. There'll be a bit more detail on when and what and how in Chapter 7.

Again, the prime thing is to put yourself in the seed or the little plant's position. (Incidentally, putting seeds directly into the garden is called 'sowing', whereas planting out little plants that have been started off in pots, probably under protection somewhere, is usually called...'planting out'. Another mystery solved...)

A seed is a miraculous time capsule, completely inexplicable to science*. It is relatively small, but the size of the seed seems to bear no direct relationship to the ultimate size of the plant. The seeds of the Giant Redwood tree are tiny. Coconuts, by contrast, are huge relative to the size of the tree they grow into. Nobody knows why this is.

Seeds are also masterpieces of durability. Once they have dried out, they can remain alive but dormant for at least a year, and very often many years. The poppies of Flanders had been dormant for decades before they were exposed to the light by shellfire and consequently bloomed into folklore and remembrance. 'Dormant for decades...' Even a cat or a teenager can't compete with this.

So... put a seed into dry soil, and what happens? Nothing. It needs water above all else before it will germinate.

Or take a row or patch of lettuces you are planting out: small plants, who get their nourishment via the intimate contact of their tiny, tiny rootlets (almost invisibly small) with the soil around them. The medium of connection is water. If you disturb the roots of a plantlet when planting out, it has to re-establish this intimate relationship, which will take time. One way of minimising this disruption is to plant out a biodegradable unit, like a toilet roll middle with a sweetcorn plant in it, but the biodegradation you are looking for won't occur until the cardboard is thoroughly wet and weakened. Judgement is called for.

You must also judge for yourself whether or not to use biodegradable pots made from compressed peat. (There are ecological concerns over mining peat.) Or you might make your own from cones of old newspaper.

So... either way... sowing or planting out, you need plenty of water. For seed sowing, drag out a groove in the land with a hoe or the corner of a rake (...this groove is called a 'drill'. Don't ask.) and flood it with water before sowing direct into the mud, then raking soil back over it, then gently watering again. As you already know, depth is not critical, but a little seed will not want to be more than a half inch deep. Bigger seeds... greater depth. Common sense, non? There is a rule of thumb which says that you should plant a seed at a depth equal to its own size. Clearly, this is a wild approximation. Very often your soil granules ('tilth') will be a lot larger than your piddling little seeds. Not to worry. Just use your common sense and you'll be surprised at what happens... usually.

For planting out, dib holes of the required size (I'm not going to insult you by specifying size here), and yes... flood them with water. Place your plants, and flood again. We're not talking thousands of gallons here, you understand. Just enough, in the precise place, to make sure that the draining water will be bound to bring the rootlets into intimate contact with the creatures and minerals of the soil that will feed them.

It really is all common sense, isn't it? So simple...

Next, all you need to do is to keep the plants' roots moist until you are sure they have established themselves. Every plant, like any young creature, is checked by any disturbance. As an example, a sprout seedling may wilt gently when planted out, but within a day or two it will have regained its vigour if you've kept its roots nice and damp.

Once the plant is established, you need to use your judgement. Ideally, if your soil is deep and rich and contains everything a young plant needs, then you need do nothing much else for it. It *wants* to grow, remember. Your job is simply that of enabler. Deep, rich, moist soil... Just let it be and blow it a kiss now and then. Let it get its roots well down and spread out like a huge fan underground, which is what it's designed to do.

However, if your soil, like most people's, is a work in progress, you might want to water occasionally. The golden rule is 'If watering at all, do it properly'. It's no good at all to just water slightly (worse than useless actually: can you work out why?) A good soaking is what you need. Don't forget that it's not the surface that matters. It's what happens three to six inches down that counts. If in doubt, scrape a bit of soil away and see how well the watering is soaking in.

A couple of points: the roots below will more or less echo the shape of the plant above when you pull them up, but the whole system is actually a lot more extensive. A very patient scientist once calculated that a single rye plant, a species of grass, had some fourteen million roots, of a total length of... 387 *miles*.

Also, remember that water on the surface will not go straight down. It will gradually spread out in a rough cone-shape as it descends through the particles, the way a tub of treacle will spread out if you pour it slowly over the central point on the top of a metre-square cube of sponge cake. If you've never tried this yourself, I recommend putting newspaper down first and locking the dog in the kitchen.

No doubt the leaves of a plant welcome a surface wash over in hot weather, and their shapes will ensure that water runs off the towards the roots, but overall, it's a good idea to keep the soil surface drier rather than wetter. A dry surface stops moisture loss by evaporation. On the other hand, in really hot weather, no doubt the plants would welcome a gentle cooling waft of evaporating water from below. Use your judgement.

That's about it for 'watering'. I'm sure you'll have worked out that just watering the surface can be positively harmful in a dry spell as it will cause roots to divert upwards to this nice new source of water (instead of downwards, which is the direction roots ought to go). They may find some traces of water alright, but these traces will dry out pretty quickly and the energy put into growing these new rootlets will be wasted if the water supply is not kept up at the rate the plant requires it... which will probably not coincide with your own rather hit and miss watering rota.

***

People used to think that ploughing in winter would let the frosts break down any clumpy clay in the field. These days people, especially organic people, tend to think it's a better idea to keep the land covered and growing something for as long as possible. If nothing else, it slows down the leaching process of winter rains, which washes out trace elements and so forth.

Obviously, you can't grow proper crops in winter, but you can grow crops called 'green manures'. The easiest of these to manage is 'grazing rye' (not 'rye grass'). As soon as your last crop of the year has been harvested, you scarify (by vigorous raking, for example) the surface of your bed and scatter the seed by hand. This rough and ready sowing process is called broadcasting. Then rake everything around a bit. Most of the seed will get covered, and will soon germinate. It will grow big and tough enough to survive most winters until you are ready to plant and sow your new crops.

An alternative is 'mustard'. You won't find grazing rye or mustard in a garden centre, I don't think. Try the yellow pages for an agricultural seedsman, or try a specialist organic seed supplier (see Chapter 19).

Come the spring, what do you have? A patch of land whose nutrients will not have been leached away, as they will have been taken up by the rye or mustard, whose roots will have kept the soil life stimulated too. Now you just dig the green rye or mustard in: hence the phrase 'green manure'. I recommend experimenting with a small patch for your first effort, for a couple of reasons. As you will have already worked out, the green plants will not have been composted, which will throw out the balance of the soil when they are dug in 'raw'. Hence, you might want to give it a week or two to rot down before planting your crops. An interesting point is that composting gives off heat. As the bulky mustard rots, you may find you get a bit of early warmth from this process. Experiment. Maybe a row of early lettuce under some sort of protection, into an inch or two of soil over the rotting mustard? See Chapter 13 for more on protection.

The main reason you might want to start with just a small patch is that if you're trying mustard, you will find that it's pretty hard going, digging it in. A rotavator is no answer, as it just stirs the plants round, and a lot of them will re-grow. You will need to find your own appropriate answer to this problem. On the farm, I used a Turk Scythe to take off the top growth before digging, rotavating, or ploughing. A sickle or slasher would do the job fine on a garden patch. Or ordinary garden shears. Or a sheep, if you could borrow one. Mind you, it would have to be fond of mustard. Forget pigs: they'll just destroy your garden and ignore the mustard. Wildebeest? Maybe... never tried them.

So no leaching; more organic bulk turned in; and, of course, that bulk will include a little extra sunshine captured in its few weeks of slow growth. Green manuring is a good thing.

It doesn't have to be mustard. There are many other crops used or useable. Trefoil, vetch, clover or lupins (yes... lupins... but a special sort) will all collect nitrogen directly from the air and store it round their roots. Nitrogen is used by plants for growing healthy green-stuff. Dig these fellows in and you've got some free fertiliser.

If you can't get hold of any green manuring seed, don't panic. Just let weeds grow over your soil, but do get them dug in before they go to seed.

But what about breaking up the clay, I hear you cry?

The organic solution to this is rather cute, I think. The problem with clay is not that it is clay, but that it is so solid that it won't let water or air in, and it's a pig to dig. It definitely needs breaking up somehow. One way is to dig sand or even gravel into it. A better way is to let Nature do the work, by either scattering as much organic mulch or compost as you can muster onto the surface, or planting deep-rooting plants into it. The surface litter will be collected (eventually) by worms, and tugged underground. En route this will help to aerate and break up the clay.

Of the deep-rooters, a favourite is lucerne, which will reach down several feet. En route, it will collect minerals and trace elements from deep down where you never normally go. When the plant dies, the roots remain in the clay, leaving tiny channels as the roots rot, allowing some movement of water and air. Also, the nutrients they have mined for you will now become available to your own crops, via the compost heap where the chopped-off lucerne ends up.

There is a huge amount of research to be done on green manuring. You can make a valuable contribution to World Sanity by experimenting a bit on your own plot, then publishing your results on the web or in a magazine.

Just one more thing on soil and water...

Plants can feed not just through their roots, but through their leaves too. You have probably seen advertisements for magical potions that will produce about a million huge tomatoes in just a few minutes for a matter of a few pence. 'Just sprinkle on!'

The active ingredient is largely potassium, which is known to help with fruiting. No doubt the treatment works, but it's a short-term chemical 'fix', and not in the organic spirit.

Better to concentrate your efforts and money on getting more high-quality compost into the land.

Or you could try making your own tomato foliar spray. The ideal crop to make it from is Russian comfrey, especially the variety called *Bocking 14*. Buy a couple of plantlets from *Garden Organic* (www.gardenorganic.org.uk) and grow them on for a couple of years. They root very deeply and bring up trace elements and minerals from below. They make big juicy leaves which rot down very well in water, making a most satisfying stink in the process. Quantities are not really important. Try stuffing as many leaves as you can into a three-gallon bucket or what have you, and topping up with water. Stir occasionally, over the next week or two. When all is done, and the leaves have clearly rotted right down, strain the water into a can and sprinkle it onto the tomato leaves. Don't overdo it. Just wet them. Do it again a day or two later. If you want to be scientific, do every alternate plant with plain water and weigh the resultant fruits against each other. I used this liquor a few times, but unscientifically, and I reckoned it worked. I'm sure it helped the leeks as well. Try it on anything you like. It won't hurt them.

At the bottom of your bucket will be a slimy mess of leaf

gunge. Either stick it on the compost or bury it with a seed potato on top of it.

A word of caution: once you've got Russian comfrey, you will probably never be without it. So plant it in a carefully-thought-out place. It will last for decades. You might like to dig up a root now and then and chop it into two-inch lengths as thick as your finger. Each one will grow into a big plant. You can then scythe or shear or sickle them down a couple of times a year and chuck the leaves onto your compost, or give the wildebeest a treat.

Nettles stink even more than comfrey if you rot (technically 'ret') them in water. So it must be good stuff. Pick them, or perhaps better, shear them when about a foot high, and still young and vigorous, with no sign of their little ribbons of tiny flowers. The juice is said to be high in nitrogen. Use it particularly on leafy crops, like cabbage, salads and chard. Not heard of chard? Details to follow in Chapter 11.

Again, there is a huge amount of proper research to be done on this sort of thing. Is nettle water even better if mixed with comfrey? Or with dock leaves? Do cabbages like garlic water? Do onions prefer nettle cocktails? What sort of quantities for best results? And what about timings? Morning or evening? Wet weather or dry? When young or when maturing? New moon or full moon? (...and no, I'm not joking. Wait till you get to Chapter 17...)

Fun for all the family. Scientifically-minded kids will love it, especially the nasty pongs.

I was delighted but not surprised to recently read that someone has taken to marketing a slug repellent based on garlic. Garlic was a pet crop of mine and I always knew it would be good against some sorts of pest, even if only for sprinkling on double-glazing salesmen from a bedroom window. Try it yourself. Grow your own garlic first and mash up a few of the less beautiful cloves in a pint or two of water. Dilute to taste and sprinkle over the lettuces you think might be most at slug risk. Be observant. Maybe just watering in a circle around the whole patch will do the job? Maybe it needs to be on each leaf, and repeated after rain? Maybe it doesn't work at all? Maybe it needs just a twist of... lime zest? Orange peel? Vinegar? Hours of fun, like I say.

This brings us to a very serious matter. Thanks to some recent European Legislation, I am obliged to point out that despite centuries of apparently successful use, it is now *completely* illegal to make organic pesticides from rhubarb leaves or elder leaves. Don't even *think* of boiling up a couple of handfuls of leaves in a couple of pints of water and spraying the resultant liquor over an aphid infestation, along with a little squirt of soft soap (not detergent) to help out with the wettability. No, you must never even contemplate doing such a thing.

But as far as I know, *CrappoAggroChemInc* have not yet succeeded in manipulating politicians into banning us from experimenting with home grown sprays as experimental foliar feeds. You may like to try a rhubarb and elder leaf tincture as a mild tonic for broad beans, say. Quite possibly, the tonic effect would be enough for the plant to withstand any amount of aphid attack, and might even encourage those present to leave.

That's about it for soil, I think. Just common sense, really, as I say. Look after your soil, and your soil will look after you... and your children's children...

But finally...

"... and here is your starter for ten. No conferring. What am I describing? It contains a hundred million bacteria, thirty million protozoa, a million algae and a further hundred million fungi? Have to hurry you I'm afraid..."
'Er... Norfolk?'
"No, not Norfolk. Don't be stupid."
'France?'
"The answer is 'soil'. For a special fifty point bonus, How much soil?"
'Europe?'
'Don't be stupid. The answer is, of course, one ounce. That's

as much as might fill an egg-cup; not that any of you ignorant trolls would know what an egg-cup is. Well... do you?"

Those numbers are approximate of course. A chemical farmer's soil will contain far fewer little lives. Organic compost will contain rather more. The complexity of their interactions is beyond human comprehension. What do we think will happen to them if we feed them raw chemicals instead of complex biological material? The same thing will happen to them as would happen to human beings: drug addiction, leading to enfeeblement, and possibly to death.

*If you think I'm wrong here, or would just like to pursue the matter for your own interest, please see the last chapter (*The Tale of the Kale*) in *Scenes from a Smallholding*, in which I examine in some detail what a seed is and is not (see Chapter 19 for more details).

chapter 6
The Square Yard Garden

The 'square yard' here is meant to indicate an area and not a location. It's just a little bit of fun to help you to work out what and how much you can grow in a one-yard square of land. If you'd like to upgrade it to a square metre, well that's fine.

Beginners at gardening often get hung up over quantities of seed and crops and how much space they need. We'll look at this in more detail in the next couple of chapters, but just for now make yourself a one square yard space on the carpet or table top or bed, or whatever. It doesn't need to be precise. Then collect about a dozen or so CDs and a few assorted books and beer mats to represent different-sized plants. Then decide what crops you think you might be able to grow in this tiny space. How will you do this? Well, by using your common sense. How big is a lettuce... roughly? About a foot across? If you've never seen one in the wild, but only the poor dears that have been packed up nice and neat on a supermarket shelf, you'll only have seen the heart, which will be about half the size of the whole lettuce; maybe less. Incidentally, the most nourishing parts of the lettuce are the parts that get thrown away by *Crappo*, meaning the greener outer leaves. Green is good for you. Deep green is better.

So if a whole lettuce is about a foot across, how many can you grow in a three foot square? Stick a few CDs or books down on your nominal square yard, and juggle them about a bit...

Nine? Probably. You could cheat and have the leaves overhanging the borders, in which case you might squeeze in a dozen. That's a lot of lettuce: well over a week's worth at the rate of a whole lettuce per day, every day. Good rich soil could just about do that for you. Imagine what croppage you might get off a standard allotment of one sixteenth of an acre: that's a patch of land of some 300 square yards/metres. A whole bunch of lettuces.

If you use the delectable and quick-growing *Little Gem* variety, at six inches apart, you can crop even more. Experiment...

In practice, you may not get such a high yield. Crowding plants up so tight isn't always a good idea. They need a bit of air space around them, and although they will compete well for available food, there must be a limit.

Now look at your square yard again and think of... ohh... how about cabbages? How big is a cabbage? Actually, they resemble pieces of string in that they come in all sizes. Spring cabbages are small and conical, and about the size of a lettuce. A cow cabbage on the other hand is huge and corrugated and can be a metre across. So, as ever, 'it all depends...', but I guess you would expect to fit between one and three on a square yard. Maybe up to 3.142 on a square metre, which is slightly bigger. (Or is that 'pi'?... which leads one to wonder how many pies would fit on a square metre. Plenty of room for experiment in organic gardening.) But I digress.

Courgettes? Just the one plant of any variety, although, if you cheat by letting the huge leaves reach over the boundaries...

Spuds? What do you think? Again it depends upon the variety, but roughly speaking, two plants. Does that sound about right? Of course, by now you'll be feeling frustrated that your patch is so small. That doesn't matter. We're just getting used to looking at a finite patch in a calculating way, the way every gardener has to, every time.

Onions? Leeks? Carrots? I guess you'll be getting pretty good at guesstimating now, but you may be surprised at what I have to say in the next couple of chapters.

The humble radish? Have a serious attempt at this one. You know roughly how big a radish plant is, and you will now have some sort of feel for how much space a plant needs. So... how many can you grow in one square yard?

PAUSE FOR QUICK AND ROUGH CALCULATION...

If you came up with something between forty and eighty, you would be about right. And if you think of the three inches extra you get down two edges if you have a square metre, you might add another dozen plus.

Part of the endless fun of gardening is seeing how much you can cram in. More in the next chapter.

All of gardening is a matter of consideration, planning and compromise. A little like 'Life', you might think.

You need to first of all decide what crops you definitely want to grow, and how much of them. Various parameters will help you decide. Spuds, for example: they take up a lot of space in your 1 sq yd. They will be delicious, of course, but that same yard would keep you in salad for several weeks if you work it right. Lettuce is dearer than spuds... lettuce needs to be very fresh; spuds don't... so maybe lettuce is a better bet than spuds?

Courgettes are not especially nutritious. You can manage without them. They take up a lot of room...

Swiss chard, on the other hand, although fairly land hungry, is packed with vitamins and far too expensive to buy if you can even find it. (More on chard later. No, I haven't forgotten.)

You will also need to pay close attention to timing. Remember your dozen lettuces coming all at once, and no time to eat them all? But you could still get your dozen lettuces off your sq yd if you plant out three or four at a time throughout the summer. The rest of the space you could use to grow something more long term. And you'll soon learn that every time you cut a lettuce you are leaving an empty space that can support either another lettuce or a few radishes.

You'll know you're properly on top of things when you are certain you will have a lettuce available *every* day of the season, if required. It takes a bit of organisation, that does.

I hope this little exercise has helped you to look at your plot in a constructive way. Every plot is made up of square yards. Each one of them can be set to intensive work if you think it through carefully, yard by yard.

A couple of further points:

From which direction will the sun be shining onto your square yard? And your plot?

Sunshine comes from the south. As summer progresses the sun climbs higher in the sky, meaning longer days and shorter shadows. Why does this matter? Obviously, longer days mean better growing. What about the shadows?

Something we haven't considered so far is the third dimension. Tomatoes grow into fairly vertical plants; so do peas and broad beans; sweetcorn is very tall; some beans are climbers. This means that you can get extra mileage from your square yard, but only if you put the tall plants to the north side of it where their shadows won't fall on the shorter carrots and lettuce.

Which of the above plants would bring the greatest return on your square yard? I would rule out sweetcorn: too big and land hungry for a small return, even with beans twining up them, Red Indian-style. Tomatoes might be better in a greenhouse of some sort. Peas bush out rather and you don't get a lot for the space they need. Climbing beans (up poles) are the obvious choice. Either good old runner beans or a variety of climbing French bean. More on this soon.

(And if you have a big tub elsewhere in the garden, decorating the front drive or a strip of naked concrete, you might like to try growing a few runner beans in it.)

Once you have fully exploited the possibilities of three-dimensional gardening, you might want to explore the possibilities of 4-dimensional gardening: growing in a world of infinite volumes... where you could, presumably, run a whole farm on the head of a pin. A fascinating prospect.

The other thing we missed out when considering the economy of the square yard was the need for paths on a proper plot. More on this in the next chapter.

Meanwhile, you could do worse than to set up a real square yard patch on your own plot, as a permanent experiment, juggling with spacing and timing. Can you increase your return from it, year on year? I'm not sure how you'd measure the increase. Crude poundage wouldn't quite do it, would it? Maybe 'money saved' compared to a shop price? Maybe calories harvested? Or maybe simply 'by rule of thumb'...Who needs to measure *every* damn thing, for heavens sake? Am I a machine?*

As a matter of interest, I've read of a gardener who takes this sort of thing seriously, and who does measure every damn thing. He reckons he can harvest 8-9kg of carrots from one square metre (13-16lb from one square yard). Or the same weight of runner beans. Or onions. Or 6kg of *Webb's Wonderful* lettuces (nine big juicy plants...) which he follows on with nine *Hispi* cabbages. All on one metre. Well-tended soil is *amazingly* productive (see Postscript for more examples).

How much would 8kg of organic carrots cost you in *CrappoMultiMax*? Or six truly whopping great, absolutely fresh organic lettuces?

And how much did it cost you, in time and money, to cultivate, sow, tend and harvest them all from one square metre of soil?

*No.

A couple of words on digging, which apply to any size of plot.

If you are faced with a really wild patch, or just a plot that has become a little overgrown, I suggest you take your time, and do it right. Rough any-old-how digging will cause heartache later on.

What you need to end up with is a patch of clean soil which you can rake into a level growing area with *no* weeds. What is the most efficient way of achieving this, given that you are faced with yards of nettles, docks, buttercups and all manner of grasses, including occasional tussocks the size of a small dustbin? Also possible razor-sharp trip-wires in the form of brambles?

First of all, walk every inch carefully and remove every half brick and old bike. Think how you might be able to recycle these, especially the bike. You could stand it on end and climb a couple of runner beans up it, couldn't you? And hang a decorative potful of pansies from the handlebars, out of the way of the slugs.

Next, you need to take down the top growth somehow. This is because you will eventually want to use your spade to chop out chunks of sod and invert it, thus preventing light from reaching the greenery, which will prevent it from re-growing. Once properly buried it will not re-grow, but instead will rot down, providing nourishment for all the billions of tiny critters your plants depend on. The snag is that one single wisp of greenery that is not completely buried is all the plant (usually a grass of some sort) needs. Within a week or two it will be roaring away again.

Thus, it all needs carefully 'topping' so this can't happen.

It may be time-consuming, but a good sharp pair of garden shears is very effective for snipping down grassy and wild-flowery bits. That sheep might help, if you can borrow it again. You might even reduce the occasional tussock to a horticultural crew cut. Don't worry about all the chopped off stuff, unless it's full of seed heads. Try to remove as many of these as you can, or they'll be up and at you next season. A little hygiene now can save literally years of weeding later.

Don't worry too much about getting to ground level with the big tough weeds like nettles, brambles and docks. They will need special attention later.

The trimmings (minus seed heads, which should be disposed of on a bit of scrap land somewhere) will not be a problem now, but you might like to rake them up for the compost. This will also enable you to see more clearly what you are faced with when digging.

Next: the Big Ones. Brambles are the toughest. With all the looping tentacles trimmed back, you can now drive your spade in all round the base and gradually lever and chop the 'crown' or 'growing point' out. Don't worry about chopping through side roots. Leave them to rot where they are. Don't forget that you will be able to get more force behind a small spade than a big one. Stay alert to the strains... be careful not to break it.

Once you've levered the brute out, bash off as much soil as you possibly can, then dispose of it somewhere where it can't be a nuisance, roots upwards. Let it dry out and die, and eventually you can compost it. It might take years to rot down, but rot down it will. Nature never wastes a thing.

Don't worry about the crater you've just made. Just back-fill it and try not to break your ankle as you stumble across it. The digging process will level it all off, near enough.

Docks have a central growing point as well, but rather than being a tough grabber of the earth as a bramble is, the dock sends down a deep 'tap root', which brings up nutrients from below. This tap root is thick and clearly full of energy, like a parsnip or carrot. If you just slice off the leaves, the root will re-grow more leaves very quickly. You have to excavate docks. Usually, it's enough to go about 6 inches deep, as any root deeper than that probably won't be truly viable. As you did for the bramble, dig round the plant, (a fork might do the job if the soil is hard) then gently lever the spade backwards. This will snap off the tap root, or, if you're lucky and careful, it might pull it all out, like a cork from a bottle. Again, bash and shake off as much soil as possible, and leave the root exposed somewhere. In farm sales or at rural boot fairs, you might come across a tool with a handle and a blade which ends in a v-shaped notch with a curious-looking length of tubing welded crossways onto the back of it. This is a 'dock lifter', as used on farms everywhere in Victorian times. The bit of tubing is a fulcrum which you lever the root against as you lean the tool backwards and pop the deep root vertically upwards.

Nettles survive by building up a network of extremely tough yellow roots, like electrical cabling, which sends up new shoots here and there. To get rid of the plant you need to scuffle around, loosening soil over a wide area and then extricating as much root as you can, like an appalling varicose vein. Don't be over-obsessive, though. Anything under 2-3mm can be left. Again, leave the root to dry out thoroughly, then add to the compost.

Finally, find (by experiment) the best grip for slicing with the spade, and slice off the chunky stuff from the tops of the tussocks, at ground level. Half a dozen firm whacks from different angles will probably do it. The roots left behind won't be a problem when you've inverted them. If slicing is too energetic, then excavate as per docks. Dynamite is not normally necessary.

This will all have taken quite a time, but it will make the actual digging a doddle, and meanwhile you will have got to know your patch rather well.

There are two approaches to digging. You can either dig a trench one 'spit' wide (a 'spit' equals the width of your spade) across one end of your patch, piling the sods somewhere out of the way till later. You then dig your next row, tipping and inverting the sods into the trench, and revealing a new trench as you go. When you get to the last trench, you fill it with the sods put aside from the first trench. Voilà.

Alternatively, you can just get on with it, inverting each sod into the hole you've just dug it from. This is quicker, but trickier. There's definitely a knack involved. By definition, it *will* fit, if all the sides and angles are true (which they never are) but only just. If you enjoy learning new skills and are prepared for occasional bouts of quite unwarranted swearing as your sod lands sideways, yet again, and needs to be hauled out and manually inverted and possibly stamped on, this is the way for you. Honestly, it doesn't take long to learn, and is worth pursuing, I would say. You may disagree.

The actual digging action should be slow and methodical. For the first sod of the first row (the hardest one, you'll be glad to know) you use the spade to chop down a couple of inches on all four sides of the sod you will be lifting out. Then dig right down at the appropriate near edge. Force the spade down, to about three quarters of its blade; more if you like. Lean the spade backwards, lift the sod, and casually drop it back into the hole, totally inverted, with no trace of greenery apparent. There. Easy... Proceed similarly to the end of the first row.

All subsequent rows will be easier. Don't forget to chop out markers an inch or two deep to delineate the sod for lifting. If you don't do this you'll end up with all sorts of ragged messes which will make more work for you in the long run. Slow, mechanical and methodical, does the job best. You can work up an enjoyable rhythm once you've got the hang of it. You may even choose to compose a work song to help with the rhythm...

'CHOP that dirt, and SLICE it down;
LEVER back, and LIFT it up;
TURN the spade and FLIP it over.....
Go DOWN, you sod, go down.
Go down, you sod, go down.'

Perhaps other allotmenteers will choose to join in. Before you know where you are, someone will start dancing, and within a matter of weeks the *Dig It Festival* will become a regular occurrence. Next stop Glastonbury.

Don't panic if the odd bit of green is still poking through. A quick chop with the blade will see it off. But don't get into the habit. Always aim for a neat perfect inversion. It's quicker, and you don't need to chop too much. Try to minimise the chopping anyway. A bisected worm does not grow into two worms. It just dies. A little more on worms in Chapter 15.

It's also worth noting that it's worth breaking yourself in gently. Digging uses muscles you may have forgotten about, but you'll remember them all right when you wake up the following morning, stiff as several boards and can't reach to put your socks on. Wives will be called to help, children will gawp, dogs will snigger. The lesson will be learned.

Don't forget to keep looking at the soil as you dig. Is it patchy? Does it look rich?

What wildlife do you see? Slugs? Toads? Beetles?

Incidentally, cutting back all that top growth will have given due warning to much of the larger wildlife. This means your chances of slicing a helpful frog in half are much reduced.

What about using a fork? It all depends on the soil and the amount of weed. If it's just a light dappling of grass say, on last year's bed, well a fork will probably be fine. Dig methodically, as per the spade, although you obviously won't be digging out marker slots, and pick up each weed as you come to it. Knock off the soil and chuck the weed onto a pile ready for the compost. But common sense says that trying to use a fork on the sort of bramble-ridden jungle we've been talking about above, except possibly for a bit of dock-levering, means a short trip to madness and gibbering despair. Use a spade.

Just for the sake of thoroughness, there is actually a third way of digging a plot, but you're not going to like it.

You systematically slice off the top sward, one turf at a time, and carefully invert each one onto a long stack. You eventually end up with a low organic Hadrian's Wall effect, useful for delineating a boundary of some sort and for sitting on to eat your Mars bars. Eventually this folly will rot down into quite a lot of semi-compost which you will then have the fun of humping about all over the plot to put back where it first came from, but not before it has sprouted a thick moquette covering of yet more grass, which will, guess what?... need digging off and somehow dealing with, possibly by forming another Hadrian's Wall.

Told you you weren't going to like it.

Chapter 7
Plots, Beds and Diseases

This chapter's title sounds a bit like a history of Restoration Comedy doesn't it? Can't be helped.

Here goes:
No two plots are the same, so it's a bit pointless me offering detailed advice on land use without seeing your own patch. It's better to internalise a few general principles and go from there, don't you think?

We've already established that the prime aim of organic gardening is to literally get to the root of things. Get the deepest things right, and the rest will follow; just like with kids. Troubles and challenges to health may be the lot of all creatures on this Earth, but strength at the deepest level will be a boon when resisting attack, and a powerful aid to recovery. In people, this means healthy inputs into bodies and minds; in plants it means healthy sowing procedures and healthy soil.
We've had a look at soil already. So what about sowing?

There are no great mysteries here. Seed is sown either straight into the soil or into trays or pots, under protection of some sort, to give the plants a head start for when the weather picks up. Clearly, plants which need a long growing period will benefit from a head start under protection, as will plants which are a bit on the delicate side (or 'Southern Jessies' as we Rugged Northerners like to think of them). Anything which has been imported, like runner beans, tomatoes, squashes, sweetcorn, and potatoes which originally came from South America count as literally southern wimps, given to curling up and dying at even a suspicion of frost. To give them a fighting chance, they really do need to be started under shelter. Let's call this procedure 'pre-sowing'. (Spuds are a bit of a special case: more in a while).

You will appreciate that there is a fair amount of inspired guesswork in pre-sowing, which can be what separates the

Good Gardener from the Bad, or indeed the Ugly.

You need to become a bit of an expert on your local weather. Not an obsessive, but you will need to know when you have a good chance of a planted-out tomato not being frazzled overnight by a frost. You might like to invest in a 'max-min' thermometer to help with this, or you might rely on something you find on the local news or the internet. If it works, use it. A gardening diary will be invaluable in future years.

As an intelligent being, you will have noted that you need to know how long a protected seed takes to a) germinate, and b) grow to a size suitable for planting out when we think/hope all risk of frost has gone. When do you pre-sow?

It won't surprise you to learn the there are no hard and fast rules here. We're dealing with Nature, right? 'Rules' get broken all the time. Nothing beats experimentation and keeping a diary. *Your* garden or plot is unique. It could quite easily be a week before or a week behind the bloke in the next street. I'm not kidding. It's all about microclimates and careful observation. You are in for a lot of fun...

The good news is that we're not talking split-second timing here. A couple of days either side of the nominal ideal will be fine... but it *can* go wrong.

It became a great comfort to me when I was learning my trade that courgettes which we planted out a fortnight later than some which had gone in just before a cold snap (but not an actual frost) soon caught them up and began to crop at almost the same time. The key is, as with kids again, not to start too soon with something, and then have them stressed and disappointed.

Again, the tomatoes...

Let's assume you have a pretty good idea of local temperatures, and have found a germination time for tomato seeds (clue: it's about ten days), and judge that if you sow in mid-April the plants will be big enough to plant out on May 30, with a very good chance of beating the frost. Hard luck. A 'completely unseasonal' frost killed all your seedlings. However, being a thoughtful rather than a mechanical gardener, you have pre-sown another dozen seeds one week later than the first batch. If you're really on the ball you will have sown a short sequence of half a dozen seeds at three-day intervals. Late frosts will never defeat you...

This all sounds a bit tough on all those poor seeds that had to die, but that's how Nature works. Remember all the seeds from the apple tree in chapter two? How many will ever get to grow? Most probably, not one. But some seeds from some trees will get planted, and thus the species continues. It's natural selection in action, with Man doing much of the selecting.*

Let us assume for the moment that you've decided what crops you want to grow, how many of each type, and what varieties, and have decided which ones to pre-sow, maybe on a windowsill or in your home-made cold frame. Windowsills are fine, incidentally, as long as they have plenty of direct sunlight. If a plant needs to search for light it will become leggy and feeble and may not survive in the wild. The plantlets you are aiming to produce will be stocky, strong, and radiant, and well able to stand up to the full rigours of a British summer; not like those poor pale ghosts you see for sale on the High St which have been reared on chemicals to make them grow quick and big. In fact, if you look at them with intelligence, the poor things look feeble, flabby and very badly stressed.

There are three ways of pre-sowing.

1   **The solo pot system** : You can give each plant its own little pot (as per the sweetcorn in the toilet rolls). This is most suitable for either large seeds, or for plants that are programmed to grow big. Large seeds include sweetcorn, beans, courgettes, and coconuts. Plants which will grow big include tomatoes, peppers, beans and aubergines. The advantage of 'solo-potting' is that if you are held up by bad weather when you were planning to plant out, the little plants will not be getting their roots tangled up with everyone else's in a too-small tray (see below). If necessary, you can 'pot them on' into larger pots until it's safe to plant out. In extremis, you can keep potting them on and eventually just haul them outside onto the patio, decking, garage roof, belvedere... The snag then is that they will need watering, a lot and often.

You can buy little plastic pots quite cheaply, but I favour making your own from those *Crappo* fruit juice cartons. Cut them in half (yes, across the middle; no, not down the length... no no no... *not* diagonally...), punch a couple of small holes in the bottom to let excess water out, and fill with compost. Being rectangular, they fit really neatly into any sort of carrying tray.

The advantage of traditional circular pots is that they are better at releasing the plant with its 'root-ball' when it's time to plant out. You hold the pot on its side with one hand, and slide the stem of the plant between your big fingers on the other hand. Then you tilt the pot so it's bottom-up, and tap it. The root-ball (usually) drops as a fragile cone onto your other palm. If there isn't enough root system, some of the compost falls off. This isn't really a problem. If the plant has become 'pot bound', through being in the little pot for too long, the roots may have expanded so far and so tight that you need a couple of horses and a hammer to yank the pot off at all. As you might imagine, square pots are less likely to bind the plant (because they are square, and root systems are round) but are quite likely to have the 'loose compost problem' when planting out.

Of course, if you buy yoghurt in little pots, all your problems are solved. Just don't forget the drainage holes in the bottom.

You can make endless free pots from rolls and tubes of newspaper, lightly glued together. Try a simple flour and water paste. It might last long enough to do the job. Experiment! Design your own origami version, possibly with two little wings and a nodding head.

An elegant but more costly solution is to buy polystyrene potting trays. These are the same size as a standard seed tray, and come in various depths, with varying numbers of cells/holes in them. A good all-purpose one has eight cells by five, and is about two inches deep. Each cell is big enough to cope with most seeds, except for the really big ones. Tomatoes are fine.

You need to be careful when filling these units with compost as it's all too easy to only half-fill the cells at the edges and corners. Likewise when watering. Edges and corners can get overlooked when you're in a hurry to get the cat out of the piano again. I don't know why you keep that cat, really I don't.

You also need to know in advance how you will get the plantlets out of the cells. If you get the timing spot on, they will drop out with a gentle tug. If they get at all pot-bound, you may need a pencil or a suitable dowel, depending on the size of the cells, to give them a helpful poke from below. Always water well before removing any plant from any cell or pot (or tray...)

2   **The traditional tray system:** This works remarkably well, if you can tolerate the disturbance and damage to the root systems when planting out. It can be a pretty root-ripping business. Amazingly, the plants usually survive it.

All you do is to fill a seed tray (or something else that will serve the purpose: ie, a tray/box about two inches deep, with drainage holes in it, and which won't fall apart when wet) with potting compost, and either dib individual seeds in at regular intervals if you are a Techno-obsessive with a tidy crew-cut, or scatter them loosely across the surface, if you are a Romantic with flowing robes and locks. Lettuce is traditionally sown in these trays, just scattered on and well watered, perhaps with a sheet of glass left on top of the tray for warmth, and protection against evaporation, and of course, a vengeful cat. I'm not too keen on this system myself, as you are likely to sow far too many lettuces all at once. Much better, I think, to sow half a dozen at a time in those polystyrene cells, every Sunday, after breakfast, *without fail*. That might be the tricky bit.

3   **The 'multi-sow' system:** This can be used with either a tray or individual pots. I would say polystyrene cells are ideal, especially for certain crops like onions or leeks, which have suitably small seeds. Instead of dropping one onion seed into a cell, you drop three. Assuming they all germinate, their single green antennae will get plenty of light and water to feed them. At planting-out time, just ease the whole 'ball' out of the cell and plant it. Bingo... three onions instead of one. And believe it or not, they won't mind it one bit. True, they will be all forced up against each other, and will have two slightly flattened sides when you come to harvest them, but what do you care? In fact, those flattened sides will make them easier to slice, will it not? Just leave them a bit of extra room, and you get three for the work of one. You could try it with four seeds (yes, it works),

and if you would prefer to have a hundred middling onions rather than fifty huge ones, experiment with closer spacing. Same with leeks. You might even sow half a dozen spring onions into a single cell, every three days. You should thus have a handy bunch of little onions all in an easy-pick bunch ready for all those crispy fresh salads you'll be making.

I've never tried multi-sowing with tomatoes for reasons which I hope will be obvious. You could try it with carrots, though. Instant mini-bunches. Very good. There are better ways for carrots, though... see Chapter 11.

Beetroot seed is unusual in that usually every 'seed' is actually a multi-seed. That's fine. Let them grow all cosied up. No problem. Is there?

If 'yes', don't forget that you always have the option of 'pinching out' the weakest of the three in the cell, thus allowing the fittest to survive. Personally, I've never seen the point in this. Apart from anything else, it means more work. Just leave them be... if the weakest beetroot Must Die... well let it, in its own time. Alternatively, pick it when it's got a bit of leaf on it and stick it in a salad or a stew, leaves and all.

That's it for sowing. Timing matters; so does temperature. The best you can ever do is plan sensibly, with at least one back-up plan, and hope for the best. You are ultimately in the lap of Nature. Be guided for timing by your seed packets, but apply your intelligence as well.

Any sort of sowing system needs the same sort of watering: compost should *never* be allowed to get dry; nor should it get water-logged. Use your common sense. Better to over-water, if the drainage holes are clear. But best is to just keep everything nice and moist.

I guess by now you will be roaring 'Yes... yes... But what about this potting compost you keep mentioning? What is it... *exactly*?'

Seriously, I wouldn't worry too much about this. I would buy a big sack of Potting Compost from the garage, and do what it says on the wrapper. Seeds are incredibly resilient. Slight imbalances won't worry them. Don't get caught up in the mainly-manufactured technicalities that the marketing people want to ensnare you with. Just plant the seeds and watch, take notes, and wait...

It is possible that you will eventually want to really explore the mysteries of seed nutrition, in which case I wish you Godspeed, but meanwhile... keep it simple. There are much more important things to occupy you, like enjoying your life, and getting the kids to sow the curly kale. They'll be queuing up to eat it later, don't you think? 'How many crinkles can you count?'

***

I know we're leaving the timings for sowing and planting out rather vague. More in the next chapters. It's very simple. It's really the twin principles of 'How do I avoid the frosts?' and 'How do I ensure a useful succession of crops?' which matter. And obviously, neither of these can be answered in absolutely mechanical terms. Common sense plays a huge part, as ever.

***

Meanwhile...

Having decided roughly how much you will require of which crop and when, there are the pressing problems of 'Where do I plant these crops, and how?'

Firstly, 'How'?

Roughly speaking, you have three choices: either randomly, in rows, or in beds. Beds are usually rectangular, but there is no reason why yours should not be elliptical or paisley-patterned if you so choose.

Randomly can be quite pretty, but can encourage disease (see below) and can be difficult to keep tabs on. Not really recommended, but by all means drop the occasional artichoke or Swiss chard into the flower beds. Or mix a few carrots in with the wallflowers. Just don't overdo it, and keep it varied.

In rows is the traditional way, and the method assumed in most gardening books and on the backs of seed packets. Easy to keep track of where each crop is; easy to access for weeding and watering; plenty of air space...

There's only one problem, really: for someone with only a small patch, it is very wasteful of land, as each row has a path beside it, doing nothing except growing weeds and getting compacted every time you walk up and down it, which makes it that much harder to dig next year.

A side effect of being land-wasteful is that it means you also have to do more digging than you need to (all those paths...). Hence...

In beds is the best system. I'm amazed at how many people don't grow in beds when it is far and away the most efficient and easiest way to raise veg.

A bed is a strip of land as long as you want it to be, and between three and four feet wide. It may be narrower or wider according to your own body shape. The idea is that instead of having a path between each row, you grow several rows down the bed with just the one path on either side, allowing you to lean in to sow, plant, weed, water and pick. Easy. And how much land have you saved by doing away with all those paths?

What's more, as you never tread on the bed, it doesn't get compacted. Therefore, once you've got the bed-soil up to scratch, you need never dig again. Except that you will of course, as you will no doubt be green manuring. But the digging will be much easier than it would be using rows. No compaction, see?

Apart from the green manuring, all you need is a bit of hoeing, using a *proper* hoe, and a bit of hand-weeding where the hoe won't quite cope, like hard up against an onion... and that's it.

If your soil is a bit shallow, you will get a little more out of it by digging your paths down a few inches and scattering the topsoil onto your nice new bed. Much better there than being trodden on. And if you have any sort of back trouble, the

extra couple of inches less to stoop will be a boon to you. You
might like to consider sinking boards round the bed to stop it
slumping back.

And... if your compost heap is a long way away, you can just
drop your weeds into the path, where they will half-rot if you
keep treading on them. No, not jumping up and down: just
walking.

Another great benefit of beds is that you can plant much
closer on them. For example you can grow eight rows of carrots
up a bed forty-five inches wide. They will grow to full size
perfectly happily, spaced along the rows as normal, which
means about 2-3 inches apart: 'virtually touching'. They grow
so densely that after one (maybe two) early weeding(s), the
foliage overshadows the soil so much that weeds don't get a
look in. You will be astonished at how many excellent carrots
you can grow on one bed if the soil is good.

I reckon you might manage a ninth row if you really work at
it. Experiment. Some varieties will be better at growing closely
than others.

You don't need to stick to long thin rows if you have beds.
For the sake of argument, let's say that the optimum space
between onions is six inches. If you have three traditional
rows, with a path between each row, you need about four feet
of land-width (say four inches for the width of the onion, plus
a foot for a path, all multiplied by three). If you plant in a bed,
reducing the space between rows to six inches, with no paths,
this four feet shrinks to about thirty inches (work it out for
yourself). This is a huge improvement, but if you look at this
scenario from above, you'll see that the plants will become
a little squashed as they expand towards each other, while
leaving quite a large patch of earth in the middle of any group
of four. Now then...

Imagine a row of twenty 'five-spot' dice. If each spot
represents an onion we have in effect three rows of twenty
onions, with the middle row displaced by 50%, have we not?
That displacement maintains the optimum distance of six
inches, but with no wasted space at all. Go for it. You might
even find yourself yearning for a suitable dibber to speed

things up and to keep the spacing tidy. Helpful diagram on page 78... but I'm sure you can come up with a better design yourself.

To put it another way: you can plant onions 6in apart each way, forming six rows up a bed 45in wide (planting 3 inches in from the edge of the bed). A 20ft long bed holds about 240 'sets' (more on sets in Chapter 11). In a good onion year the crop will average six ounces or more each. That's about 80lb (about 40 kilos) of onions; that's well over a pound, or half a kilo of onions per square foot. And the only reason to plant them so far apart is so you can hoe (using a *Swoe* or similar) between them. They could be planted 4in apart and would produce an even heavier crop, but of smaller onions which would be fiddlier to weed. And, of course, if you multi-sow in cells, you can save a fair bit of labour in all this. (One drawback of multi-sowing is that onions, like garlic, need to ripen in sunlight after they stop growing. This gives them the protective papery skin. But if pressed up close, that papery skin won't develop so well. Be flexible, and not too greedy, is a handy rule.)

Obviously, most gardeners are not as obsessive as a commercial grower is about optimum use of land, but it seems to me that if you can grow 200% of your normal crop for 120% of the work, then it's daft not to do so.

If a small garden has, say, a 6ft by 4ft patch allocated for onions, the gardener can choose to either plant the old-fashioned way, in rows, or the rational way, in a bed. Planting 6in apart, in rows 1ft apart, he will expect to harvest about 48 onions. Planting 6in both ways, he'll get 113. There's no competition, is there?

I know for a fact that at this point some dear soul will say 'But I don't want 113 onions. It's too many.' There is a rational solution to this problem.**

As another example, beds are ideal for planting courgettes at virtually double the normal spacing. In fact, it seems to me that beds are ideal for everything.

***

Now it's time to mention another organic principle: 'rotation', meaning 'systematically circulating certain classes of vegetables around a number of beds'. Here's how and why:

Crops are susceptible to pests and diseases, just as people are. If a person lives in an area where malaria is endemic, he is probably going to get infected. It's the same with plants, except that they don't catch malaria; not yet, anyway (but who knows what money-making wheezes *CrappoGenoTec* have up their polyester sleeves?).

Also, it's possible that a person might eventually build up an immunity to the local diseases, as might plants; but likewise, you can bet that the diseases will also mutate and thus return, as deadly as ever. People can't always choose where they must live, and neither can plants in the wild, of course (they just die out); but as gardeners, we can play our part in helping our plants to avoid disease by not growing them on the same patch year after year.

Avoiding troubles by careful thinking and planning, rather than spraying troubles with nerve toxins whenever they appear, or whenever we are terrified that they *might* appear, is very much a part of the organic method and approach. Paying attention; observing; thinking; planning; experimenting...

Long experience has shown that a four-year rotation is effective in preventing the spread of most soil-borne plant diseases. It is not foolproof, however. Intelligent vigilance protects potatoes just as much as it protects our children.

The standard four year rotation groups vegetables thus: potatoes; legumes; brassicas and roots to be planted on Patches A, B, C, and D respectively. We'll look at each one of these in the next four chapters.

Meanwhile which sowing system would you say is going to make rotation a doddle? Random, rows, or beds?

Random is hopeless... you'll never keep track of where you planted what last year, never mind five years ago. The odd specimen or tuft in the flowerbeds should be fine, though. Just keep your eyes peeled.

Rows will work well, as long as you have your plot mentally

quartered into Patch A,B,C and D.

But of course, beds make rotation *easy*. If you have only limited space, Bed A will be Patch A, too.

The beds (or rows) don't have to be straight. Curve as you wish. Stick a forty foot spouting dolphin in the middle of each one if it will help with the watering.

The only important thing is to keep the beds mentally separated, so that you don't plant the same crop on the same bed, every year. The Vale of Evesham used to be famous for its onions, year after year. But, unsurprisingly, an onion disease gradually built up in the soil until it was virtually impossible to grow onions there at all. Rest the land by not re-planting the same crop, and the disease doesn't get a chance to get established. Common sense.

The rotation in practice:

Year 1: plant spuds on Patch A; legumes on Patch B; brassicas on Patch C; and roots on Patch D.

Year 2: spuds shift to Patch D; legumes shift to Patch A; brassicas shift to Patch B; and roots shift to Patch C.

Year 3: spuds shift to Patch C; legumes shift to Patch D; brassicas shift to Patch A; and roots shift to Patch B.

Year 4: spuds shift to Patch B; legumes shift to Patch C; brassicas shift to Patch D; and roots shift to Patch A. But you were expecting that.

That's it. In **Year 5,** the cycle begins again.

Spuds, legumes, brassicas and roots are the four standard 'groups'. For onions, salads etc, read on...

*Yes, yes.... Or 'Woman'. OK? Let's not make a big thing about this.

**It is entirely possible that my arithmetic may have gone askew in the preceding paragraphs. Please don't write and tell me. I don't care. The point is made, correct arithmetic or not. And anyway, you should have better things to do, like making elderberry and blackberry jam from local hedgerows, or teaching your children how to fire peas or home-made stink bombs from a catapult at any sort of itinerant garden pest that catches your fancy.

Chapter 8
Patch A: Solanaceae
[That's spuds, mainly]

This is going to be a short chapter... very simple stuff.

The rotation system is based upon the fact that plants belong to families. And members of each family tend to be susceptible to the same diseases.

The Patch A group, *solanaceae*, is really all about potatoes, but tomatoes, peppers and chillies belong in this family too.

Five procedures for spuds: chitting, planting, earthing, lifting, and storing.

Chitting: A neat and tidy little word, around which many amusing double entendres may be constructed. It means 'sprouting'.

First of all, work out how many spuds you'll need to harvest to last you through the winter, maybe up till March, or even April if they keep well for you. Calculate how often you eat spuds, and roughly what weight you need per meal.

Balance this against the cropping rate you might reasonably expect, which will be something between a pound and a kilo per foot of row.

Obviously, you now need to know what the right spacing is to define this 'foot of row'. Here goes...

There are two main categories of potatoes: earlies and maincrop. There are also 'second earlies' which are intermediate.

Earlies are quick growing, which means you can crop them early, at about a pound per foot-row. But they crop relatively lightly, and don't store as well as maincrop. Who cares? There is nothing in the culinary world to beat your own organic early potatoes. It is the sign of severe mental illness to even think of storing them, unless you have to (see below).

Maincrops grow more slowly, but crop at about twice the rate as earlies; about a kilo per foot-row. They are the ones you store.

You can plant earlies closer than maincrop. Try about 15in between plants, in rows about 18in apart.

Maincrop do better at, say, 18in apart with about 27in between rows.

Don't forget that there is nothing magical about these numbers. They are simply some sort of observed average optima. You may find that your poor soil means the plants need more room to get enough sustenance. Or your incredibly rich soil may mean you can pack them in like radishes. Well, no, not like radishes, perhaps, but you get the drift.

Now factor in how many foot-rows your own particular Patch A will allow you to plant up.

You should now have enough information to decide roughly how many spuds you need to sow. If in doubt, buy more 'seed' potatoes than you think you'll need (see below).

I suggest that if you are going to use beds, it might be easier to stick to a couple of straight rows per bed, offset, rather than doing the clever triangulation thing as per onions. See 'earthing' below.

Back to chitting: I recommend that you buy fresh 'certified' seed in late winter or early spring from a proper garden shop/ centre rather than plant up stuff you got cheap from *Crappo* or a neighbour. Examine the new spuds. They will be of roughly large egg size, and will have little growing points called 'eyes' concentrated at one end, called the 'rose' end. Pack the spuds, rose end up, in some sort of tray and keep them somewhere in the light but away from frost. Don't let them get too warm. These are plants, not parrots. As the days begin to lengthen, the eyes magically begin to shoot. Magic is a good enough word. If you cut open a spud you will see no trace of a dark greeny-purple shoot... but it will appear anyway. After a week or two the shoots will be strong and sturdy, and obviously itching to be planted. Don't panic! What matters is to plant them only when frost is no danger. Actually, you do plant them a little earlier than the last expected frost as they will be going underground where frost doesn't reach. You just hope they won't break the surface too early.

As a rough guide, April is a good sowing time. But if it's still frosty, it won't hurt one bit to wait for another week or two. What matters most is that the plant is not checked. Just.. relax.

Planting: While the seed has been chitting, you have been busy preparing Patch A. Stick all your compost on it. All of it. If there's only a bit, dig out a 6 inch deep hole where each spud is going to go and drop the compost into it. If you've got a lot, scatter it over the surface before digging. If you've already dug, scatter it everywhere and rake it in a bit. If you have any comfrey available, cut the leaves down, let them wilt, then try sticking a leaf or two under a spud or two. The leaf is rich in potassium, which the spud will enjoy, and the greenness will rot down directly under the spud, providing a tiny amount of warmth in the right spot. See if these spuds are any earlier than the rest.

Plant each spud about 6 inches deep. You might like to dig a furrow and drop them into it, then rake back. Or you may prefer to dig little holes. Or, if you've got a whopping great spike and a very big hammer, you might like to dib individual holes. All these methods work. Pick what suits you best, and if you can think of a better method, use it. All that matters is that the spuds go down about 6 inches. Any shallower and they may break surface too early and get frosted. Any deeper and they will come up a bit later than they need to. Experiment. Maybe put half of them in a couple of inches deeper than the rest to insure against frost damage? And put in a few a bit shallower in case you get lucky?

Earthing: As a plant grows, tiny spuds develop along the root system. If the light gets to them they go green and become inedible (poisonous even...). Thus, we 'earth up' to protect them. This means hauling earth from either side of the row up into a long 'Toblerone'. Don't worry about covering the green shoots. They'll soon grow up through it. A rake is normally fine for this job, but you may prefer a draw hoe (see Chapter 4). If possible, repeat later, but it's not vital. It may be difficult to earth up properly if you've gone in for fancy triangulation.

You can use lawn mowings as an earthing aid if it suits you.

The worms will eventually tug the grass into the soil.

Lifting: Sometime in July you'll begin wondering if the earlies are ready to sample. Why not try one? After about twelve weeks of growing they should be about right. Get a fork under the whole plant, from one side, at the base of the earthing up. Go quite deep, and lean the fork backwards. Golden treasures will be revealed... Boil as soon as you like, and serve, perhaps with a wipe of butter. You needn't bother with anything else.

Maincrop takes about twice as long to mature as earlies. Watch for the flowers. When they appear, the plant has stopped growing. When the stems begins to wilt, it's *definitely* lifting time. The longer you leave them in the ground, the longer they are susceptible to disease or slug damage.

Lift as for earlies. You may like to borrow a larger fork for this job. Dig deep to one side and lever back. Don't worry if you spear a few. They'll mash just as well as the perfect ones. But you will enjoy the feeling of genuine competence when you are skilled enough to lift a whole row without spearing a single one.

Wait until you have a decent sunny day for spud lifting. They need to dry off before packing.

Storing: Examine every spud as you lift it. Is there any pest damage? Small holes, a millimetre or two across, are probably caused by wireworms. This is quite common if your plot was recently grassland. Larger holes of 5mm or so are probably caused by slugs. Don't worry. Holes aren't poisonous. Just put all damaged ones to one side, to be used as creatively and deliciously as possible as soon as possible.

It seems to me that the most economical procedure for lifting goes like this: carefully lever back and expose the tubers of the first plant; shake the soil from the tops (the 'haulm'), which you put to one side; gather the spuds up into a loose collation. Collect every single spud from the plant, even the tiny little ones, as if there is any disease in the soil, tiny spuds can carry it as well as big spuds can. Anything under a quarter inch can be gashed with a finger nail and chucked into the nettles, or thrown for a gullible dog to catch.

Leave the spuds in a loose huddle to dry off for a couple of hours.

Move on to the next plant and repeat.

By the time you reach the end of the row you should have a pile of haulm ready to dump on the compost heap, and a series of rosettes of shiny new potatoes drying off and gleaming in the sun. Go and have a cup of tea.

Next, you will need three or four paper sacks and a small bucket or tub. Your greengrocer will have some old sacks. Turn them inside out, and voilà... new sacks. If you don't have a greengrocer any more, try the convenience store or even the supermarket. Or use big cardboard boxes or trays which you can exclude light from, but which can 'breathe': ie, not solid plastic.

Next, examine each separate pile. You are looking for four categories of spud. Firstly, any damaged ones. They go into a sack marked 'Use First'.

Next, you are looking for next year's seed. Use your head. If one plant has produced a mass of small potatoes, and another has produced only three, but whoppers, ask yourself whether you want to use these as seed? Next year you may be raising a whole mass of tinies, or just a few brick-sized jobs, depending upon how the genetics work out. Personally, I don't pick seed from these plants, but by all means give it a whirl if it suits your tastes.

If you're looking for a spread of spud sizes, then pick one or two seed-sized specimens from each pile that you think has performed well. Obviously, you will know by now how many seed you will need to select. Add a few more for insurance.

These all go into a sack marked 'Seed'.

This leaves 'Proper Spuds' to be sacked and labelled as such; and the tiny marble-sized ones. These go into the bucket. When all is safely gathered in, you rinse the soil off the tinies and deep fry them, wondering why people waste their *time* on pretentious restaurants serving *Pommes de terre bouillées, hachées, et totalement terrifiées* drizzled with a *coulis* of tender young rhino horn, never mind their money. Those deep-fried tiny tatties are one of the highlights of the culinary year.

Keep the sacks of spuds in a cool/cold place, out of the light. Commercial growers go to all sorts of lengths to prevent their stored spuds from sprouting too early. All you can do is keep them cool. They will begin chitting when they feel the time is right. Keep an eye on them. Rub the little sprouts off any remaining eaters (but NOT the seed). They will then keep a bit longer.

You might like to tip out the spuds every couple of weeks to make sure there is no disease spreading through the sack. Try as we might, it seems that our farm can never escape potato blight. We practice excellent hygiene, even dumping diseased haulm down wind of the growing area and never composting it, but we still get it every year. It seems to blow in off the Atlantic ocean, believe it or not. Or maybe Pembrokeshire? However, as always, there is a solution. First of all, we grow earlies and second earlies rather than maincrop varieties, as they mature before the blight arrives in force. A favourite is *Maris Bard*.

But try as we might, some blight gets into the sacks. So we need to tip them out and remove the nasties and yukkies every now and then.

You will probably see a couple of tiny green 'tomatoes' growing on an occasional plant. These are the fruit, derived from fertilised flowers, and they contain true seeds (the tubers we plant are not true 'seed' of course). When you've found your feet, you might like to experiment by letting one of these fruits mature, then drying off the seeds on a piece of paper. When you sow them the following year, any plant that grows will be a new variety of potato. If you plant on the tiny tubers that result, you will get a crop that differs from the 'seed' you originally bought in. Will your new variety be any better? Who knows? But every variety you can buy in shops has been developed in this same way, by patient and curious people such as yourself. There's half a chapter about such a person, called Luther Burbank, in *The Secret Life of Plants* by Bird and Tompkins. If this book doesn't amaze and stimulate you I'm afraid you are already clinically dead. Best get used to it, and let this book slide gently from your grasp....

It's just possible that the haulms and seed pods of potatoes might make a suitable plant tonic as described in Chapter 5. The poisons might stimulate the plants' defensive systems to the point where the bugs choose to leave, or become so tired that they remain, unmoving, on and around the points of infestation, possibly for months on end. Experiment. But be careful: poison is poison.

Varieties: There are dozens of varieties available. New ones turn up every year. Some will be fractionally earlier than other earlies; some will be slightly more disease resistant; some will crop slightly more heavily; some will work slightly better in more acid soils, and so on. What you will never find is The Perfect Potato. Gains in one direction will probably mean a loss in another. What you need is something that works for *you*, in your climate, soil type, etc. This takes time to decide on, but gardeners are patient. If you're not already a patient person, you will become one after a year or two of working to Nature's rhythms rather than Mammon's. Worthwhile things take time.

As a matter of principle, I would start off with some old-fashioned tried and tested varieties (see Chapter 12). If you have space, try just one or two plants of other varieties. Do this every year and pay close attention. Very soon you'll find what suits you and your plot.

You might also ask other gardeners what they plant and why. Wander round some allotments and ask the people there. Even ask in the garden shop: 'What do you sell most of?' and 'What grows best round here?' It all helps.

If you fancy something fancy, contact *Garden Organic* and find out when they are holding the next of their famous Potato Days, when people scramble over boxes of exotic spuds in not quite as unseemly a manner as at a *Harrods'* sale, but not far off it. More on *Garden Organic* in Chapter 19.

A final wonder. The eyes of potatoes are their growing points and, amazingly, if you're careful you can rear an eye into a plant. During World War Two the Americans helped out with Britain's potato stocks by shipping over thousands of 'seed' in the form of eyes. These were carefully cut from the main potato, being sure to keep a chunk of the starchy tuber attached as a food source, like a yolk sac for a tadpole. These were carefully grown on into proper plants and helped to feed the country.

It is obvious from this that you can save money at planting time by cutting your chitted tubers in half, or even quarters, keeping a sturdy sprout on each. Experiment.

Once I had a spud that escaped under a table in a shed and produced an enormous long white shoot, with spidery little roots attached. I separated this from the wizened little raisin of a tuber it had grown from, and planted it. I was amazed when it grew into a modest plant, spuds and all.

Try a couple of tomatoes or peppers on Patch A, if you like. Even a chilli if you're feeling bold.

Give half of them a bit of protection, and compare with the unprotected ones for cropping, earliness, etc. Perhaps you could make a 'tube cloche':

Stick 4-6 bamboos 4-5ft high in a rough square, pentagon or indeed hexagon, and wrap a 6-7ft length of bubble wrap round them. Poke bits of wire through the wrap to tie round the bamboo. The fine green-plastic coated stuff they sell in £1 shops is good for this. (See jolly helpful diagram in Chapter 13.)

Make sure the bubble wrap can be opened for ventilation, and lift the wrapping an inch or two off the ground, too. Make sure bees and insects can easily get in to pollinate the flowers. Leave the gap in the bubble wrap downwind, otherwise the wind will blow it all apart. You can shut the gap up for the night to keep the plants warm using clothes pegs, bulldog clips, or whatever.

Keep a keen eye on things, and constantly ask 'How can I improve on this, preferably using only intelligence and junk?'

***

In Year 2, the spuds move onto Patch D, recently vacated by the roots. After three years without it, this Patch will be very keen to receive all your compost again, to bring it back into good heart.

Chapter 9
Patch B: Leguminosae
(means beans, mainly)

Another short chapter.

It's not a hard and fast rule, but experience shows that the two major dressings an organic grower uses, compost and lime, are best applied to the potato patch and the bean patch respectively. The compost feeds the greedy spuds, while the lime serves two purposes.

Firstly, it helps to reduce the acidity of the soil. Don't get too concerned about balancing acidity, but if you can get hold of a few pounds of ground limestone, scatter it over the surface of Patch B and rake it gently in. It will slowly release its active ingredient with the rain.

The second thing lime does is to combat a brassica (cabbage-tribe) disease called clubroot. However, it works better a year after application. Thus, as brassicas will be moving across to Patch B next year, this year's bean patch is the preferred place to scatter it.

The members of the legume family that you will be mainly concerned with are French beans, runner beans, broad beans, and peas.

What they have in common is an extraordinary capacity for extracting nitrogen from the air, thanks to bacteria in nodules on their roots. This nitrogen, which is much in demand for leafy plants (like next year's incoming brassicas), is later released into the soil when the plant dies. Thus, at the end of the season, don't uproot the old plants. Just cut off the haulm with shears and compost it, and leave the roots to slowly release the nitrogen for the cabbages.

Let's assume that you're using beds of between 36 and 45 inches wide. Each bed will probably have room for just two rows of peas, a couple of feet apart. Maybe you can squeeze

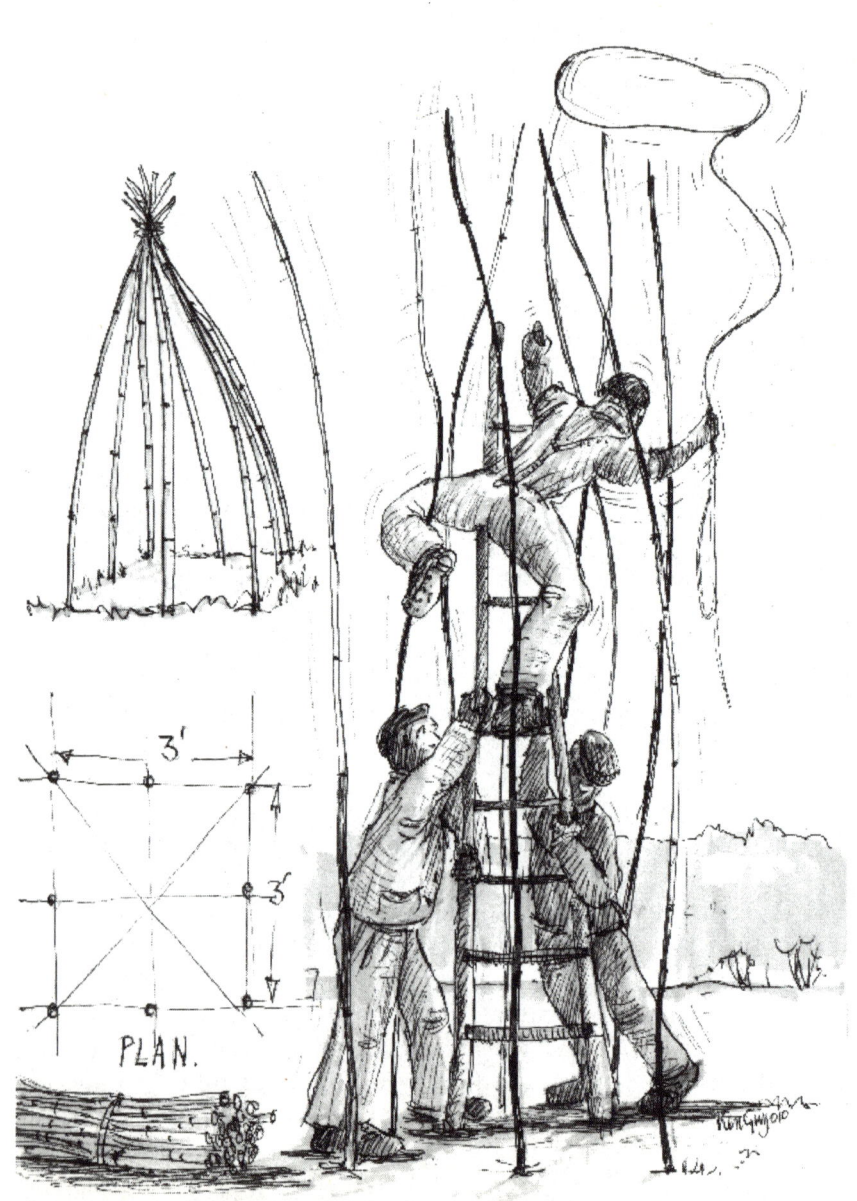

PLAN.

a third row in? Maybe? The trouble might come with the picking: having to squeeze along a narrow space, and then bend down, getting hopelessly snagged up in the foliage. Could be there for days... cups of tea dangled in from precarious bamboo fishing rods... chips forced through the vine mesh one at a time on sharpened sticks... even summer nights can be surprisingly chilly. Perhaps best to not go there.

Whatever, it's unlikely that you'll ever have enough space to grow enough peas for your total requirements, as nothing disappears more quickly from the kitchen table than a trayful of peas in pod. Even our dogs used to love them and would snatch them out of buckets and snuffle them out of plastic bags. Maybe the smart thing is to just leave them available to whoever fancies a handful, and not bother cooking them at all. Fresh and raw... the best way for peas. They taste even better, of course, if they've been pinched off the kitchen table.

So, resigned to never having enough, the best way to grow peas, I suggest, is up a length of pig mesh. This is 4 inch square galvanised wire mesh, strong enough to deter a mild pig, but light enough to handle, and easy to erect in the garden with a bamboo threaded down through it every three or four feet, then rammed into the soil (see caution below). The traditional method for sowing peas was under a light thicket of hedge twigs which not only gave the little plants' astonishing tendrils something to grip onto to haul the stem upwards, but also gave some protection against birds digging the sprouting seeds up. Pig mesh offers no such protection, but it's easier to get hold of for most people, quicker to erect, almost indestructible and easy to shift around and store. You could always scatter twigs around the base of it, or something else that might deter birds if they are a nuisance to you.

Chicken mesh would do a similar job to pigmesh, of course, but it will drive you nuts trying to pull all the bits of haulm out of it at the end of the season. Pigmesh is easy. Zzzip... done.

Once your mesh is up, rake out a drill on either side of it. How deep? Do you need to ask? Yes, an inch or two. It's not critical. Interestingly, you can sow them more closely than you might imagine. Just rattle them into the trench from your hand, aiming for a plant every 3 inches or so. You don't need to be precise. I've sown them at 2 inches apart or even closer and they don't seem to complain.

If you are likely to suffer from critter trouble (birds, mice or voles, mainly) then sow pretty thickly. Animals are opportunistic rather than thorough, and a few of your peas will get through, whatever the depredations. You might try rolling the peas about in a little paraffin before sowing. Not even mice like paraffin sauce. Or you might try pre-sowing your peas under protection in lengths of guttering, carefully liberated from a builder's skip. Fill the guttering with soil or compost and sow the peas; keep them properly watered. When they're well established, just slide the whole mass off the gutter and into the waiting well-watered trench. Mice won't fancy them once they're properly growing.

If you are short on space, you might like to consider growing a mangetout pea. These have been bred to have large pods and small peas. You eat the whole pod. Delicious, especially in salads or stir fries. And no wasted pods, of course.

Similarly with runner or French beans, which tend to crop more heavily than ordinary peas. And as you eat the whole pod, you get more vibrant crop weight per seed planted.

Runners grow tall and have pretty flowers too. I think the best way to grow them is in wigwams. Push in four big bamboos (7-8 footers) about a foot apart down the most northerly edge of one side of the bed, then match them with four on the other side. Add extra bamboos across the bed to join the outermost pairs of the two previous sets, again, about a foot apart.

Assuming your bed is 3 feet wide, and if my sums are right, you will now have marked out a roughly three foot square, using 12 poles. Right? Now the fun begins... and you'll probably need an assistant. I always do, anyway. Pull the tops of all the springy twangy poles together (see what I mean?) and tie them together to form a wigwam. Eventually, sow one or two runners beans at the foot of each bamboo. The second bean is an insurance. That's 24 beans per wigwam. When they grow, they will get pretty crowded at the top, but that doesn't really matter. You'll be concerned with picking the beans from the lower reaches.

Of course, you can make the wigwam longer, narrower, or wider, according to your own needs and available area.

Alternatively, you could go for the traditional method of two parallel rows of poles, tied across in pairs, with a reinforcing bamboo tied across the top cruxes. This works fine, but takes more work, I think. It's also vulnerable to sudden summer gales. Whoop! Wooosh! Whole lot gone... blown flat, possibly crushing an innocent child. Wigwams let wind pass between them and are sturdier anyway. Your judgement.

A word of caution. Whenever you are forcing bamboos in, always wear good thick leather gloves. Bamboo is very tough, but as it ages over the years it becomes more brittle. If one should snap with all your weight behind it, it will make a frightful mess of your hand. Be aware of where your face is, too... keep it out of line with the bamboo at all times. If your soil is a bit on the tough side, you might like to find a suitable metal spike, a couple of feet long, that you can hammer in to make holes for the bamboos to drop into. There. Easy. Now try getting the spike out... It keeps you fit, does gardening.

You'll be sowing the seeds direct, a couple of inches or so deep, as you suspected, in May and/or June. You might like to try raising a few extras in pots to replace those which a critter pinches. Or you might like to go the whole hog and sow the lot in pots. One wigwam should give you 10lb or so of beans; maybe more.

Pick them on the young side, so they don't develop any ropey string down the spine. By trial and error, you'll soon find how long they can get before they become stringy.

If you have a glut, be grateful, and get to work freezing them. Blanch them for 2-3 minutes first, as with any veg you are freezing.

Try them raw, too. Give them to the kids as juicy lollipops.

You could leave a few pods on the plants to develop for seed (see Chapter 14).

Try mixing the runners with climbing French beans. They don't crop as heavily but make a bit of a change. Some people think them 'more refined'. Well, yar boo.

If you want to mix it a bit more, cut the width of the wigwam by a foot, and run a row of dwarf French along the sunny edge of the bed. The climbers won't shade them there.

Of course, you can do this along the sunny side of the pea patch too. Plant the Frenchies at 6-9 inches apart. Experiment.

Broad beans are different. You can actually sow some sorts in the autumn and they will stand out over winter. I've never found this to be a great advantage though. It seems to me that it just makes them vulnerable for longer. If you fancy trying it, plant them into the space left by the new potatoes on Patch A. The rest of the beans will catch them up when the next season starts.

The good news is that you can sow them earlier than runners in the spring as they are so hardy. Sow them a couple of inches deep, and experiment with the spacing. Try triangulating them at 9-12 inch centres across a length of the bed. If they are a dwarf variety, they may plant even closer.

You can either eat them pod and all when very immature, or just the beans when properly swelled up (pick one to try, now and then); or you can leave them to mature and dry off on the plant, before storing as dried beans for winter soups and casseroles. Some will serve as seed for next year, of course.

Be sure to admire the exquisite packaging that the pod offers the beans. It's a sort of fleecy fur... amazing stuff. Crash helmets should be lined with it.

That's about it for beans. If you should hit a long dry spell, squirt some misty water over the runner bean flowers. Might as well treat the Frenchies and peas while you're at it.

There are a few words on varieties in Chapter 12.

Chapter 10
Patch C: Brassicae
(Cabbages and Things)

Yes, another short chapter!

Brassicas are mainly cabbages and cabbagey-looking things, like kale, broccoli, calabrese and sprouts. They all suffer from the same pests and diseases, of which the worst are probably aphids, white butterflies, root fly, and pigeons; not to mention rabbits and slugs. We'll be looking briefly at a few pests and diseases in Chapter 15, but for the moment suffice it to say that cabbages are pretty keen on them. Vigilance is needed.

The ones to start with are, I suggest, cabbage, kale, and broccoli.

Cabbage: Essentially three types: spring, drumhead, and savoy. Also 'red', which is like green cabbage, only red, and tends not to crop as well. One of the great graces of brassicas is that you should be able to be picking something all year round.

Drumhead, red and savoy: Savoys are the wrinkly version of cabbage. They tend to be bigger too, and a little hardier, I think. The seeds all look identical and get easily stuck under your fingernails. Patience...

Either sow them out direct in springtime (not recommended as they are 98% certain to be eaten by something unspeakable the *moment* they emerge. Make that 99%), or pre-sow them in pots or cells. I would go for pre-sowing every time. First of all, you can do it even if it's bucketing down outside, in a corner of the shed with the *Goldberg Variations* or *Da Gangsta Hoodboys* tinkling in the background. Dog at feet, possibly. Mug of tea. Maybe a pair of tweezers and a saucer to simplify the problem of little round seeds rattling all over the place and

spilling onto the floor when you rip the packet open.

Sow one to a cell, or two if you're feeling a bit ruthless, and intend to cull the weaker seedling when they all germinate. If you're using standard 'shop seed' rather than more expensive 'grower seed', you may well find that quite a lot do not germinate or come up all sizes. This may not be a problem though. Remember the F1 seeds? As a gardener, you really don't want fifty identical plants maturing at once. Some big, some small, is better for you.

Cells can dry out quickly. Make sure you're on top of keeping the watering up to scratch.

When the seedlings are a couple of inches high and looking sturdy, they are ready to plant out. Maybe plant on a dozen or so, into bigger cells or pots, as back up?

Use your common sense when planting out. Leave 1-2ft each way between the plants. Triangulation is fine. If you plant them closer you will get smaller cabbages. You might like to experiment with planting quite densely, even at 6 inches, then cut out alternate plants when they get big enough to be worth picking. Cutting at the base is better than uprooting (try shears, or failing that, bolt cutters or a hacksaw), as you don't want to disturb anyone else's roots. Leave the other plants to grow on to become full size. When you cut a full size plant you can try cutting at the base of the cabbage head, then cutting a cross into the top of the stump. For some reason this seems to encourage regrowth. Some weeks later you may find three or four leaf clusters the size of large sprouts. All good stuff, but maybe you'll prefer to just uproot the stump, bash it with a hammer to break up the woody parts a bit, and chuck it on the compost. This will free up the land for a green manure or a 'catch crop' (of which a little more in Chapter 17).

Spring:
Usually sown in summer or autumn to over-winter and provide some valuable greens in the 'Hungry Gap'. Once you've been growing your own food for a year or two you will deeply appreciate what a problem the Hungry Gap used to be to subsistence farmers and peasants. Before freezers and cheap global transport, people had to rely on local crops. These were

plentiful in late summer and autumn, but there came a time in late spring when there was either nothing left, or what was left had run out of steam and was beginning to rot, and the new harvest was still months away. Hungry days.

I think you could say that a truly good gardener is someone who knows he/she'll have some greens to eat next week. You could make that a target if you fancy a challenge.

If you can offer some protection in the coldest weather, springs will appreciate it.

A couple of words about cabbage in general, which will apply to other brassicas too...

Pre-sowing is not only more convenient, but it also offers a good head start. Cabbages are very vulnerable when they first germinate, and there seems to be a long queue of God's creatures who would like to share them with you. To a pigeon or a rabbit a just-sprouting two-leafed seedling is a nice bite. Thirty or forty make a pretty decent snack. To you, this means a whole crop wiped out. However, if you plant out sturdy seedlings, some will probably survive. Probably.

The moral, of course, is to find a way of dealing with rabbits and pigeons. A little more on this later, but it's mainly a matter of commonsense physical deterrence and protection.

Another good reason for pre-sowing is that you beat the weed problem. Seed sown directly has to compete with the Professionals, which will smother your little darlings as soon as possible. Hoe the bed clean just before planting out and you're ahead of the game.

We don't really speak of 'greens' any more, do we? Even lettuces, which used to be green are now white 'icebergs': juicy but tasteless. The cabbages in *Crappo* are usually just the pale hearts.

Of course, the true value of a cabbage lies in the very part we throw away: the green leaves. They are tough, naturally, but it seems a terrible shame to chuck them out and then buy vitamin pills. Even the toughest leaf will gradually break down if chopped fine and simmered for long enough. Try making a modern 'hay box'. Boil up your stew or whatever, then leave it to slowly simmer on, using its own heat, in a highly insulated environment: this used to be a box full of hay, but is now a box insulated by or made entirely of junked polystyrene packaging. Your local hardware store should have mounds of it that they'll be glad to give you. Try zapping a few roughly cut leaves in a food processor of some sort, to break the tough stuff down a bit. Then tip the goo into the stew.

Juicing will also get a lot of the good stuff out of tough green leaves.

Kales & broccolis:

These tend to be quite substantial plants which need up to a couple of feet between them. Again, closer means smaller. Experiment with what suits you and your plot best.

You grow a kale for its rich green leaf and a broccoli for its immature flower heads. Of course, you can eat the broccoli leaves and the kale flower heads if you wish, but they are not so well developed.

If you plant enough of them, kales and broccolis should keep you in greens until May the following year. Personally, I don't think you can ever have too much of them.

Sprouts:

People tend to have views about whether sprouts are a food suitable for humans. Their two main advantages I think are that they provide some greens in the depths of winter, right through to spring, and that they tend not to be so damageable by varmint. People often take off the 'Brussel top' as a small open cabbage. Taking it off early is said to encourage the sprouts themselves to bulk up. It's a tasty bite.

Sprouts can get pretty tall, so they might need staking, especially in a windy area.

Others:

Radishes are the obvious 'other brassica'. You don't need to restrict them to Patch C though, unless you know you have a serious soil-borne brassica disease problem (more in Chapter 15) because they grow too fast (5-6 weeks; maybe faster) to succumb to most cabbage-ills. So you can drop a few seeds in anywhere you find an empty space. The trick is to do this every week, not just when you think on. Having said that, you will no doubt find that some seed sown a week later will catch up with an earlier batch. There are no mechanical rules in gardening. Keep observing. Keep a diary. Keep thinking. After a couple of years, you'll have got it more or less cracked, but you'll also know you'll never get it perfect. Well you can't, can you? Nature is in charge. In June 1975 it *snowed* in Derbyshire and put paid to a cricket match.

Speaking of cricket... kohl-rabi is worth a try, perhaps. It grows to the size of a cricket ball, with occasional leaves poking out of it. Eat the leaves and the ball, which is an inflated stem. Finely sliced, it makes a crisp and refreshing raw nibble. If you enjoy them you might reconsider throwing away the stems of cabbages and sprouts. Why not cut them open and scoop out the soft and juicy centres? Chuck it in the stew.

Turnips and swedes are much maligned vegetables, it seems to me, in this effete age of chocolate-dipped sea urchins, hazed with balsamic strawberry vinegar on a seared bed of Himalayan squid. But they are great in casseroles and stews and soups. Easy to grow, too. How deep to sow them? Well, the seeds are indistinguishable from other brassica seeds, so I'll leave you with that one. And how far apart? I'm sure you will have internalised by now that closer means smaller. Thus, a 4 inch turnip will need an 8-9 inch growing circle. Agree? If you like your turnips smaller, you know what to do. Swedes grow bigger, and require a 10-12 inch circle.

Both crops will triangulate well. You might care to sow them direct, an inch apart (roughly). Critters will eat a few of them, but you'll be left with most of them... probably. When they've got to a size which looks as though they might be getting a bit cramped, thin them out and eat the thinnings, leaves and all. You may care to pan fry them along with a few shavings of parmigiano reggiano, in left-handed yak fat over a glowing nest of sequoia charcoal, but somehow I doubt it. Chuck them in the stew.

I wouldn't bother with cauliflower until you've had a year or two's experience with growing more basic brassicas. Caulis can be a bit disheartening; but with a couple of years' successes under your belt, you will no doubt soon be ready to try anything. Excellent.

***

Brassicae is a large family which includes mangel wurzels, rocket, and, surprisingly, wallflowers. It also includes a couple of weeds, most commonly charlock and shepherd's purse. Normally these are not a problem but if you have land contaminated with clubroot (Chapter 15) you should hunt them down and destroy them with extreme prejudice, as the CIA would say, as they will carry the disease on their roots.

Get a wildflower book (see Chapter 19).

People say that sprouts grow better if planted in firm soil. I expect that's because if the soil isn't firm the plants will blow over. Try it and see. Obviously, you won't be over-keen on stamping flat your carefully cultivated beds. 'Improvise and observe'.

See Chapter 12 for a few comments on varieties.

Chapter 11
Patch D: Tutti-rutti
(carrots, parsnips)

This chapter is a bit of a cheat, because it's pretty much of a rag-bag, and not exclusively concerning 'roots'.

However, roots will probably be the largest part of this Patch's concern, so let's start with them.

Carrots:

As mentioned before (Chapter 7), you can grow an awful lot of carrots on a smaller space than you would imagine. Do a bit of pre-calculating, as per potatoes, and then balance your ideal quantity of crop against other uses this Patch will be used for (see below). Organic carrots are so different from the pale and scurvy-looking candles they sell in *Crappo* that I do recommend growing as many of your own as you can. If you grow 'too many', you can always juice them and freeze if necessary, also freezing the de-juiced residue as a basis for many a winter soup.

Again, I'm assuming you will be sowing into a bed. It's essential to hoe the bed clear of all weeds before you start. Use a hoe or rake to scrape out shallow drills about 6 inches apart, and water well. Aim to sow the seed about 2-3 inches apart, but don't lose any sleep over it. If in doubt, sow closer. Rake the soil back over and tamp it down firmly with the rake head. Then water again, but gently, or you'll wash all the seeds out into a little pile at the bottom of the bed.

The seed is very small and pretty annoying to handle, especially on a breezy day. It just needs a little patience, and an understanding that it really doesn't matter if three seeds fall into your drill where one was intended. You can always stir them about with the rake later if your aesthetic sensibilities are too outraged. Or you could try mixing the seed with a cup of dry sharp sand, then using a teaspoon to deliver the sand/seed mix to the drill. Or you could try mixing up a pot of non-fungicidal wallpaper paste and stirring the seeds into that. Sow the paste mix either immediately, or when the seed has just begun to germinate.

No, I don't really fancy these methods, either. I did once get as far as buying some paste but before I'd opened the packet I realised that all the time I'd be spending on mixing could be better spent on sowing. I'd already wasted twenty minutes in buying the paste. And anyway, how would I do the sowing? With a teaspoon? An icing bag? A grease gun? By the roughly hurled handful, stucco-style? I could foresee an awful lot of sticky messes. Again... time wasted. Best to just sing a sunny song and get on with it.

> The sun has got his hat on,
> Sing Hip Hip Hip hooray!
> I'm happy sowing carrots
> Though it's going to take all day.
> (Shimmy left; shimmy right)
> It's a happy sunny day!
> Hoy!

When to sow? The little seeds take about ten days to germinate, and are surprisingly tough. Mid-spring is worth trying. It's also worth trying later sowing too. In our case we sow in June, which is normally thought to be too late. We get decent crops though.

Why June? The answer's further down the page. (Any ideas, meanwhile? Worth a moment's pause?)

It's important to keep the little plants well weeded as soon as you think they are big enough to tolerate a bit of knocking about. This can be a fiddly business as the seedlings are so skinny and vulnerable. And it'll give your back a good work-out as you lean across to the middle rows of the bed.

If you're feeling bold, you might even like to consider flame weeding before sowing: details in Chapter 16. When the seedlings are a couple of inches high, use a hoe (a slicing hoe like the *Swoe*, not a chopping hoe like the Dutch) to slice off the weeds between the rows first. If you've let the carrots get above 2 inches tall you're making extra work for yourself, because by then the weeds will be sure to be twice as high and four times as tough. Use the edge of the inverted hoe to lean up close to the carrots and pull gently towards you. This should scrape out quite a lot more weeds, or at least rip their leaves off. Don't be harsh. The carrot roots won't welcome you hacking them about while 'helping' them. For real close-up work, use your sheath knife. Place it by the tiny carrot and pull towards you. You might find you absolutely must use forefinger and thumb from time to time, but I advise using a tool wherever possible. You may find that you need to press the knife against the small carrot to protect it as you pluck out a particularly difficult weed. Or try pinching the weed between the ball of your thumb and the blade, and gently pulling. If it is just too intimately twined up with the carrot, try a pair of scissors.

If you have sowed closely and the plants are looking crowded, either don't worry about it and be grateful that they've germinated so well, or thin them out. If you just leave them you'll end up with more but smaller carrots, which might suit you better than big ones. Bigger ones store better, though.

If you decide to thin, you don't need to leave more than

2-3 inches between the plants; maybe a little more if you're growing big ones like *Autumn King*. Be guided by the seed packet, but err on the side of closeness.

What you do need to be careful of though, is to ease the thinnings gently from the soil, creating as little damage as possible. This is because the carrot root fly, which is a wretched nuisance, hunts by smell, and a broken carrot stem is pretty pungent. You might want to put each new thinning into a plastic bag straight away, and make sure the soil is gently firmed back. Try a bit of the leaf in a pickle sandwich or a stew.

The carrot fly is the pest that causes us to sow in June. It seems that the blighters have early and late generations. If you sow in April or May, the early generation is likely to catch your crop. But if you sow in June, you might just get away with it before the late generation gets into full swing. We've found it pretty successful, and the late sowing doesn't make a huge difference to the size of the crop.

Garden Organic has an ongoing programme of research into dodges and stunts to outwit pests, and in its previous existence as *HDRA* (the *Henry Doubleday Research Association*) they discovered that the carrot fly problem could be greatly reduced by surrounding the carrot patch with a plastic barrier. It doesn't need to be huge. Something 18 inches high will be a great help. If you have any pig mesh left over, you could wire some bubble wrap, or sheet polythene onto it, and fix it roughly with bamboos. Take it down for weeding. Put it back again afterwards.

This is time-consuming and difficult, isn't it? But growing food has always been time-consuming and 'difficult' if you think of it as a chore, or your living depends upon it. That is why chemical pesticides were seen as Godsends when they first turned up. At last... Food growing was going to be cheap and easy. Nobody, apart from a few 'organic cranks', foresaw the problems we were lining up for the future; and nobody ever listens to a crank or even a visionary until the last minute, do they? And even then they try to dodge around inconvenient truths. In the middle ages beavers were officially classified as 'fish' so that monks could eat them on 'fish-only' Fridays.

So, if you want to grow the world's best carrots, you'll have to put a bit of extra work in. Personally, I see this as an exciting challenge to my ingenuity rather than a tiresome chore.

What other ways might a gardener like you and me discover for deterring carrot fly? I've never tried it, but I'm certain that a barrier spray made up from something bracing like orange peel juice, or garlic, or pine needles, or a pungent cocktail thereof, might well put a little fly off the scent pretty effectively. What do you think? There's plenty of room for experiment and personal creatively in an organic system. When you've found something that definitely works, share it with the world. You'll be doing more for world poverty and global warming by this act than by anything else in your power. If you don't see the connection, go to the end of the chapter.*

Carrots are given to creating amusingly erotic shapes sometimes. Be warned. You may wish to make an attractive blindfold for your more impressionable younger children at carrot-lifting time in the autumn (the precise time will depend upon the variety and what the season has been like).

Experiment with pre-sowing three or four seeds per cell and planting out as instant bunches. Just be careful not to disturb the roots when planting out.

Parsnip:
Parsnip seed is even more annoying than carrot seed in a breeze, as Nature has surrounded each seed with a thin membrane which acts as a sort of wing, enabling the wind to take the seeds further. Oh, spiffing... just what you need on a lively April morning when your rake's just blown away.

Parsnips (should/might) grow to about twice the size of carrots, or even bigger, so give them a bit of extra room. Use your common sense, and keep a diary for future reference. They are a bit of a pig to peel, so you really want to be peeling two big ones rather than five small ones.

Incidentally, a lot of people waste a lot of time and a lot of food and vitamins by unnecessary peeling. Why do we peel potatoes? Seriously? To clean them or to remove the tremendously poisonous skin which will poison you to death with a blue face and an unattractively protruding tongue, not to mention soiled underwear, if you should even look at it? It's just for cleaning, isn't it? And you can clean spuds perfectly well with a stiff brush or abrasive cloth. Just let them soak well first to soften the soily traces if they've been stored for a long time. If you waste, say, 5% of every spud by peeling it, that means you can save 5% on your spud-digging-planting work by not peeling, yes? Think of it as a 5% pay rise. It hurts me to see apparently sane people hacking a spud the size of their fist down to one the size of their eyeball. What's the *point*?

And apparently, the majority of the vitamin C in a potato lies just under the skin. So... do you need to peel that spud?

Same with carrots; same with parsnips, except that they really do need a bit more care as grit and muck gets into the tiny crevices, a little like sand on a beach.

That's about it for 'roots', except for 'beet', which we'll come to in a minute.

Patch D is the obvious place to grow your onions and leeks, as the other three Patches will probably be filled with single-family plants (although not absolutely necessarily so; more later). I hope Chapter 7 has laid out a simple way of planting onions. The simplest unit to start with is not seed, but 'sets'. These are tiny little onions, grown from seed the previous year, and sold by weight. All you do is to plant them out, as early as March if you fancy it. Personally, I'd leave it till a bit later. Experiment. Some now, some later. See what the difference is come August, when you lift them and leave them to dry off in the sunshine for a few hours or days. They're properly dry when the stems have withered back to a brown strap, suitable for plaiting up into beautiful, beautiful strings to hang in the kitchen, sitting room, bedroom, ... You'll want to stroke them every time you walk past.

It's a good idea to plant sets quite deep, which means with their 'noses' *just* poking above ground. This is because some birds delight in pulling them out of the ground and tossing them around. I've no idea why. Bored, possibly. Plant 'em deep and get a rubber cat to either put them off by its mere presence, or to chuck at them if you catch them at it.

Garlic:
Garlic is a delight. Plant the cloves an inch under the surface.

Leeks:
You can treat leeks much as onions for spacing. This mainly depends on the variety, and as ever, packing them closer will mean more but smaller mature plants. Leeks (and onions) sown from seed can be a real pain to weed, as their first leaf is a single tiny green stem, looking remarkably similar to the first shoot of a grass seed. It can very easily become swamped, apparently as soon as you turn your back. Pre-sowing in cells has always seemed to us to be the answer to this one.

The traditional way of growing leeks, which you might like to try, is to sow the seed into a tray, then when the plants are taller than your palm is wide (or 10-12cm, if you prefer) lift them carefully out and transplant each one into a hole dibbed as deep as your hand (say 15cm). Use any old stick as a dibber, or pick one up at a boot sale. Usually they are made from broken spade handles, filed off to a rounded point. Measure 15-18cm up from the tip, and wrap a bit of insulating tape or similar round the tool to mark it. Obviously, this isn't vital, but it can help to be sure you're getting the depth roughly right every time.

You just drop the wirey-rooted leeklets into the holes, water well, and leave them. Don't backfill. Oddly, they grow very well. The hole helps them to develop a long white stem. Don't panic about either of these measurements. Even quite small seedlings will transplant well. Just drop them into shallower holes. Make sure the top inch or so can see the sky.

Beets:
This means mainly beetroot, but also *Swiss chard*. I've given this plant the distinction of italic letters, as it is a prince among plants.

Beetroot can be treated much the same as carrots and parsnips. Remember that the seed in the packet is often a cluster of two or three. Just sow them every 3-4 inches and see what happens. As they grow, thin them if you like. Closer means smaller, of course.

We always grow a cylindrical version, which zooms slowly up out of the ground and in a tubular shape. More convenient for land economy and ease of chopping, we think. See what you think. Another plus is that beet apparently tastes sweeter in the section that has grown above ground level.

Now, *Swiss chard*: this is some sort of spinach beet, of which there seems to be a confusing number. Personally, I wouldn't bother with anything else if you have *Swiss chard*, although you might like to try traditional spinach to compare it with. However, spinach does not contain all the accessible iron that Popeye said it does: chard is better; and spinach tends to bolt, meaning it quickly runs to seed and you can't crop it any more.

Sow chard as for beetroot and thin out to about a foot apart, or 18 inches if you have the space. Chuck the thinnings into a stew (or 'cassoulet' if tu préfères) or eat in a cheese sandwich.

When the rich deep dark green leaves are a foot high, or 18 inches if you can wait that long, cut off an outer leaf from each plant, and rush to the kitchen. Chop the green crinkly leaf from the white ribbed stalk, and roughly chop both elements. Boil both parts lightly, and enjoy. Amazingly, you get two slightly different dishes from the one leaf. The green part is packed with vitamins, and has a rich nutty taste. You can hear it calling you. The stalk is sweeter.

As I write, my wife has just brought in an entire chard plant from the polytunnel she is clearing for the new season. Laid on its side, it took up pretty much of a square metre of floor space in the kitchen. Cooked separately, then re-combined in freezer bags (old marge tubs, actually) there was enough green and stem for twelve generous portions; and we'd already been picking leaves off the plant for months. I don't think any other plant can give such nutritious and tasty value per yard of space.

If ever there was one single good reason for growing your own food, it's *Swiss chard*. You'll hardly ever see it in the shops, largely because it wilts quickly and nobody wants a floppy rag of a leaf on their shiny display, do they?

If you want to persuade a friend to grow their own veg, offer them a couple of leaves of chard to cook. If they don't like it, they're a lost cause and are doomed to a life of oven chips and whingeing.

What else? Personally, I wouldn't bother with stuff like radicchio and Chinese cabbage and celery just yet, until you have had a year or two of getting the basics right. In fact, we never had much success with celery at all. This happens, you know. If you talk to a group of gardeners you'll find that Harry has a terrible time with beetroot, while Daphne never has any luck with onions. A curiosity.

Personally, I wouldn't bother with squashes on this plot (although try them, by all means) because they are much better off under protection. More on this in Chapter 13.

Courgettes:

Courgettes will grow well outside. Remember that they take up about a square metre each.

Salad Stuff:

But you will want to grow salad stuff. The good news is that salad plants don't usually belong to the Big Families (like legumes and brassicas) so they don't harbour their diseases ('rocket' is an exception, being a brassica). This means you can drop a dozen lettuces or a strip of radish pretty well wherever you can find the space. (Yes, radish *is* a brassica, but it rarely proves a problem on the disease front. But you already knew that, didn't you? Didn't you? If completely stumped check back in Chapter 10.)

The secret to lettuce growing is to sow little and often, maybe half a dozen seeds a week, in cells, under protection (see Chapter 13). If you find that some sowings zoom away and others dawdle, note it in your diary and use this information when planning next year's sowing. Whatever, better too much lettuce than too little. Give any surpluses away; or, if you can supply half a dozen *regularly* every week, you might earn a few bob from a local pub or restaurant. You really do need to be regular though or you're wasting the owner's time. Let him down more than once and he'll drop you. Quite right too. But if he likes your lettuce, and finds you to be reliable, well, who knows.... maybe he'll like your other crops. Peppers? French beans? Chillies and garlic?

Something we have found handy is a mixed assortment of salad plants, sold as a *Cut and Come Again* selection; some selections are a mix of half a dozen lettuce types; others are mixed with chicory, chervil, endive, rocket, or beet; some are sold as an 'oriental mix' with pak choi and mizuna. You sow them direct, and quite densely (read the packet). When the plants are a few inches high, trim off the tops of the leaves with a pair of scissors. Instant salad mix. If you're not too brutal with your cutting, the plants will grow up again. You'll get four or more cuttings from a sown patch. Maybe sow another patch to grow on to replace the first one? And then another?

Experiment with other leaves in salads too. Beetroot leaves, raw cabbage, carrot tops, kale, turnip... Some will suit you better than others, and some, particularly the brassicas, will benefit from being finely chopped. And curly kale, for example, can be pretty hard work even then. Cut it *really* fine! If you have any radishes that have been forgotten (it can happen...) the fresh new seed pods make a tasty nibble.

Sweetcorn:

Finally, sweetcorn: if you've never tasted sweetcorn straight from the plant, raw or lightly boiled then lightly smeared with butter, then you've missed something truly delicious. They are tall pants, which means they take time to grow. Thus it's an idea to sow them under protection, in April, maybe in old loo rolls, as suggested, or in pots. Cells tend to be too small. Or sow them direct in May and hope you're lucky.

The plants should be stationed a good foot apart, in a block rather than a row. This helps with the wind pollination. They should be ready for eating from midsummer onwards, depending on the variety. Obviously the 'earlies' won't crop as heavily.

Note that as they are such tall plants, they take a lot from the soil. Are they worth the effort? You decide.

Some ideas on varieties in the next chapter.

* World poverty:

Third world farmers and peasants have been relentlessly conned by *CrappoAggroChemInc* for decades, who have persuaded them that they should buy fancy new 'high-yielding' varieties of seeds from them which also, oh dear, need lots of expensive artificial fertiliser and pesticides if they are to actually crop at all, never mind show high yield. And guess who has the exclusive rights to sell the fertiliser and pesticides? Huge numbers of peasant farmers in India have killed themselves as a result of the poverty trap they have thus been tricked into. If subsistence farmers could grow decent crops without *CrappoAggroChemInc* robbing them blind for pesticides, by using a simple home-made potion of orange peel or garlic juice... what a difference that would make. Something published on the web will be sure to reach them, and sooner rather than later. Can you come up with something made from common ingredients, preferably organic? It just needs imagination and perseverance. There will be *something* that helps.

Global warming:

Every dose of pesticide and fungicide etc, and every shovelful of artificial fertiliser requires the use of lots of oil, both in the manufacturing processes and in the delivery systems. If a farmer, gardener, or grower, anywhere in the world can cut back on the predations caused by say, carrot fly, by using a home made organic brew... that means a ton or so less CO_2 released into the air, per farmer. There are millions of farmers in the world...

But you knew all this! Seriously... there is much valuable work to be done in back gardens and on allotments, looking for organic solutions to pest infestation of crops.

chapter 12
Varieties and Timing

I think the first thing to say after describing the classic four plot rotation, is 'Don't take this as Holy Writ'. There are many variations on the theme. And, of course, some people prefer a five or six part rotation. Others reckon a three part one works fine, especially if they're short of space. The principle to stick to always, is to not grow plants of the same family repeatedly upon the same patch of land. Disease *will* build up, and you'll probably never get rid of it. So... rotate! And the longer the period, the better.

Also, you don't need to be absolute over what to plant in each bed, as long as the principle of rotation is stuck to. For example, if it is more convenient for you to plant the onion tribe in with the brassicas, do it, but then stick to it.

Of course, when you're planning your year ahead, you might want to pay some attention to 'over-running'. For example, as you clear away the remnants of your pea and bean crop, you might want to plant part of the Patch up with a few cabbages or kales which are hardy enough to over-winter in the ground, and will serve as the advance guard for the remainder of the incoming brassicas the following spring. Again, I wouldn't recommend getting too obsessive about this sort of thing in the first couple of years. Just keep observing and thinking... As in 'Oh.. an empty space! Bother! If I'd thought ahead, I could be planting xyz into that space... Never mind; this year I'll green manure it.' You get the drift.

Incidentally, no, the 'xyz' is not a sort of Polish banana. Someone has been teasing you.

***

A lot of beginner gardeners spend ages worrying over what varieties to plant and how many of each, and how many millimetres between each one, and when and... oh, it's all so difficult, isn't it? I do understand this anxiety, as I once shared it myself, and spent ages fretting over detailed layouts and week-by-week plans. It took several years for me to shake this habit off completely.

I think the source of this trouble is the society most of us live in, in which everything has a timetable, and if you're a minute late, you miss your train and that means Alfie will be hanging around pointlessly at the other end for you, and that means he will miss *his* appointment... and dammit... you've forgotten to bring your mobile... still on charge in the kitchen... so can't ring him.. dashed out with the kids... got them to school with seconds to spare... should just make it to the station... and there in the middle of the road is a set of temporary lights that weren't there yesterday. Endlessly red... red... Time is awasting.... Come on... come *on*... Then there's an approaching siren and everything stops, everywhere... green... amber... and red again... Yaaaargh!

Punctuality is vital for most things in our lives; but it winds us up something awful.

And computers haven't helped one bit, have they?

Gardening is different. It works at the eternal pace of Nature where what matters is not split-second mechanical timing, but 'When conditions are right'. Instead of following a rule book, we need to make judgements, and it is this involvement of our creative intuitive capacities that helps to make gardening so fulfilling.

It might say 'sow in March-April' on the seed packet, but if you stop to think about it, that is nothing but a broad suggestion. The Shetlands dance to a different tune than the Scillies, for example. And anyway, it doesn't mean that the seed self-destructs at midnight on April 30.

What if it's been pouring with rain throughout March and April? It's quite pointless to sow the seeds into freezing mud. Just... *relax*. And while relaxing, maybe you could remember the old country saying that it ain't worth sowing seeds till you can sit with your bare bum on the soil. You could set up a few deck chairs and sell tickets for the charity of your choice.

And while you're still relaxing, you could do worse than to think about how it is that no matter what the weather has been like, the bluebells always seem to come through it, to flood the woodland with their cool, de-focussing hues. Seeds *do* this. All seeds. Roses bloom, perhaps a little 'late'; apples blossom, perhaps a little 'early'. But to Nature, 'early' and 'late' are meaningless mechanical terms. For Nature, plants grow, flower, set seed and die when the conditions are right: 'time' doesn't come into it. Our own lives follow this pattern too, if we do but think about it.

The only reason we get anxious is that we don't have enough faith in Nature to do the job. And, of course, we are impatient. We want it all, and we want it now. A recipe for hypertension and unhappiness, if ever I saw one. Gardening helps to restore a proper perspective to our lives: don't try to force it; go with it. Every yogi will understand.

Where has all that got us? Mainly, I hope, it suggests that your gardening should be a continuing act of joy and fun and miracles, not another calendar-mad routine which needs to have all the creativity and enjoyment ritualised out of it.

Now then...

Varieties:

Every year hundreds of new varieties of vegetables are formulated. I think 'formulated' is the word for it. They are not 'created', unless they have been genetically modified. Nor have they been 'discovered', as Man has spent a lot of time intelligently cross-breeding from selected plants in order to deliberately produce what he hopes will be a tomato with a slightly sweeter taste or a lettuce with extra resistance to *Canker yukipu,* or whatever. Some of these modifications can be quite dramatic. I believe I'm right in saying that all, or nearly all, the brassicas we grow for food have been bred from the same original parentage. This means cabbages, sprouts, kales, turnips etc are all closely related. This of course means that they are susceptible to the same diseases. It also mean that they will cross-breed very easily. More on this in Chapter 14.

There have been two main phases in plant selection and breeding, and they had different aims.

The first phase began thousands of years ago and involved wise and observant settlers deliberately fertilising the flowers of one head of the local grass with the pollen from another carefully selected plant. Over a few years, this procedure led to a doubling or trebling of the seed yield; then onwards and upwards. All our cereals (oats, barley, wheat, and rye, mainly) were derived by this method. Once they were scrubby grasses. Now they feed millions.

As society moved from warring tribes to settled economies, more people took more time to investigate what else might be derived from rough old weeds. Nobody knew about genes then, but they knew that if you crossed *x* with *y* you might just occasionally come up with something special. Most of the time you wouldn't, but once in a while, you hit the jackpot. Then you made sure you kept the resulting seeds very carefully, and planted them the following year, making sure that no stray pollen got in to dilute all your hard work. This probably meant planting your precious new seeds half a mile upwind from the normal crops. No doubt your fabulous new plants came up a treat but were then all stamped on or eaten overnight by a bear or a rabbit. But, with luck, one or two survived. Plant development is a slow business!

Over the last two hundred years or so, all the major garden vegetables have been developed in this manner, mainly by keen amateurs. This led to hundreds of varieties of runner beans, for example, with different coloured flowers, different cropping periods, greater height, better resistance to drought, better tolerance of salty winds, etc. These were often grown very locally, as they were developed by local people to suit very local conditions. Growing runners on the South Downs ain't the same as growing them in the Borders, and gardeners everywhere knew that. Seeds were exchanged and traded as precious commodities. Often, many people's lives depended upon what food they could grow themselves. Better seed meant a little more crop, which meant a little more security and a little less hunger.

The second phase of plant formulation developed over roughly the past fifty years, with the growth of cities and supermarkets and the decline of backyard veg growing. Now new varieties are formulated with the requirements of commerce at the top of the list. *CrappoDewFreshVegInc* don't want an absolutely delicious tomato that goes soggy after two days. What they want is a tom that will stand hanging about for a few days in storage, then for another week, or preferably a month, on a supermarket shelf. What it tastes like comes very low on the list. They know that after a while, thanks to their near-monopoly on a town's fruit and veg supply, the public will be gradually lulled into thinking that tomatoes *ought* to taste a bit sour and runny and of little else.

Thus we have two quite different classes of veg seed: the trad (sometimes called 'heritage seed') and the mod. Which will suit the backyard gardener the best, do you think?

We live in a *Novelty Now!* sort of society, which has been conditioned into thinking that unless you spend a lot of money on it, it can't be any good, and we are thus constantly presented with racks of new New! NEW! varieties of seed every year, each successive one promising even greater levels of perfection than the NEW!!! varieties of last year.

You can see where this going, can't you?

It seems clear to me that the trad seeds are the most suitable ones for a home gardener, particularly for a beginner, who is looking for nutrition and taste above bullet-proof skin and virtual indestructibility. The problem is that commerce is in charge now, and EU regulations on seeds have meant that it is actually *illegal* to sell certain varieties. Why they felt this regulation was necessary is a mystery to me. So what if six very similar beans were marketed under different names? Why on earth does that matter to anyone except a bureaucrat who's never seen a bean in his life?

Anyway...

The point is that the genetic variety represented in all these carefully developed local types is in danger of being wiped out. This is simply foolishness, and possibly dangerous foolishness at that. What happens for example, if everyone is forced by law to buy only *Polythene Pam* tomato seeds, and along comes a virus that just loves thick tomato skins? Ruination of the entire European tomato crop; thousands of farmers impoverished (remember monocropping?); tens of thousands of ancillary workers like drivers, packers, stackers, clerks, etc thrown out of work and onto the public purse; riots in Spain and Italy.

Yes, I exaggerate, but the principle holds up. We absolutely *need* genetic variety.

No doubt the world tomato industry would pick up again in a year or two as clever technicians discovered that if you insert a gene from an Indonesian sea cucumber, the *Polythene Pam* skin will now become distasteful to the virus, all the while ignoring the fact that viruses mutate as you watch them. The good news for the 'food' industry of course is that this sort of scenario gives them a back door into forcing Genetically Modified Organisms onto a public that staunchly and quite rightly wants nothing to do with them. 'Oh... but without GMOs we won't have *any* tomatoes! No! None at all! I mean... just *imagine* an idyllic English summer picnic, little fluffy clouds by a tinkling riverbank, kids laughingly tossing their frisbee for Sweetheart, your adorable Labrador, Dad making an amusing mess of trying to catch a fish, and Mum peeling open the Tupperware, with pastel-coloured cows in the background, and Vivaldi-a-gogo on the stereo, but with *no* glossy, juicy tomatoes! Is that what you want?'

Bah... Humbug.

The rational solution to this problem-in-waiting is to allow anyone to grow and sell whatever varieties they want to, and the more the merrier.

Garden Organic run a splendid organisation called *The Heritage Seed Library* whose aim is to preserve as much as possible of the genetic diversity invested in traditional garden veg. Obviously you can't preserve seeds by simply keeping them under lock and key for a few decades. Seeds are living creatures, and they eventually die. They need to re-grow if they are to live on. The *Seed Library* sees that this happens.

All you need to do is to accept a few seeds from the *Library*, grow them on, following the instructions supplied, and then return a quantity of your own new seed to the *Library*. Year on year, the genetic line is continued, and you personally will have a few of the threatened variety to grow for yourself and pass on to friends. And as long as the genetic diversity is still in existence, even if only in a couple of dozen back gardens, sanity may yet prevail when politicians finally understand how important genetic diversity is.

Does this mean that you should avoid new varieties? No, not at all. Just be aware that the trad varieties are tried and tested, and will probably be less flighty in performance. I would definitely recommend starting off with trads, and adding a mod here and there as you get the feel of it. Note that while the trads are tried and tested, this does not mean that they are superior to mods in all cases. Old runner strains, for example, are prone to getting a stringy backbone which can be a minor nuisance. Modern strains have been bred to avoid this. But do they crop as heavily, in most soils, in most conditions and blah blah blah? Who knows? You can only tell if they are right for you by (fun) trial and (moderate) error. If you start with trads, you will have a benchmark to work from.

How do you know which varieties are trads?

Firstly, as you might imagine, they tend to be the cheapest seed available, as they tend to be easier to grow. As ever, ask the seedsman, neighbours, allotmenteers...

The internet will be helpful too, but don't forget that advice from someone in Alice Springs may not be appropriate for Milton Keynes.

It's quite possible that you won't be able to get some (or any) of the varieties listed below. Don't worry about it. Try something else in the meantime, and keep your eyes peeled.

Secondly, here's a handy list. It is not all-inclusive:

Potatoes:
We demand an awful lot from our potatoes. We boil them and mash them, bake them and roast them, chip them and whip them, and... well, all manner of other things. In Russia they even make vodka out of them, at the rate of forty bottles per person per year. Heavens..

Not surprisingly, not every variety is *perfect* for every purpose (except possibly the vodka). Earlies are probably best just boiled, I would say, but as ever.. experiment!

We have always found *Maris Bard* to be an excellent all-rounder as an early. 'All-rounder' means it's good for boiling, roasting, baking, chipping, and salads. The maincrops below are also good all-rounders, although the *Fir Apple* is probably the best for salad use. But this isn't *Let's Cook Something Pretentious for a Panel of Drooling Free-Loaders*. It's real life! They're all fine.

Earlies: *Duke of York, Pentland Javelin, Maris Bard.*
Maincrop: *Maris Piper, Desiree, King Edward, Pink Fir Apple* (*PFA* is not a heavy cropper, and thus counts as a bit of a 'fancy'. Worth a try, though. The smaller tubers are wonderful eaten cold, skins and all, off a silver salver, watching the sun go down, with a glass of Elderberry '98 to hand and a Bach cello suite on the stereo. Hopeful-looking dog sat to attention nearby.)

Not all of these varieties will grow well for you. Your soils and weather won't suit every variety just so. But you are in with a good chance with these 'known' types. Be observant. Keep a record. You don't have to weigh every single spud. Just get an impression and note it. Examine the spuds for any skin problems, or other disease signs. More on diseases in a while. Don't worry...

Next year add a plant or two of a couple of other types, and see how they do. We once planted *Wilja* upon the recommendation of a skilled gardener friend who had fabulous crops. They were hopeless for us. No idea why.

These observations apply to all the vegetables listed below as well.

Peas & beans:

An old favourite is *Kelvedon Wonder*, an early cropping pea which can be sown in early spring. To keep the peas coming, sow more every two or three weeks, right through to the end of July. If you're more concerned with getting a full rather than an early crop, I do recommend *(Hurst) Greenshaft*. We've grown them for twenty years and have never had a dud pea. The pods fill well and you get 9-11 peas per pod... wonderful.

Here might be a good point to mention/repeat that when seedsmen speak of an *early* variety, what they mean is that this particular seed will grow and mature *quickly*. Normally, that will mean you get your spuds or peas *earlier*, if you plant them at the normal time. But it can also mean that if you plant an 'early' variety later in the season, you have a good chance of it maturing before the end of the season. Hence the multi-sowing possibility of the *Kelvedon* peas. It also means that 'early' potatoes sown in mid-summer, preferably away from possible frost later in the year, might give you a crop of fresh 'new' potatoes for Christmas.

A reliable mangetout variety is *Oregon*.

A trad broad bean is *Windsor*. So is *Sutton* (a dwarf variety, thus less likely to be flattened by a passing squall, or indeed Irish Wolf Hound). Sow in mid to late spring (ie, not over winter).

Try *Czar* as a runner, or *Scarlet Emperor* or *Painted Lady*.

Climbing French: try *Blue Lake White Seeded*. If you can't find it, just go for the one that gives best value per seed and go from there next year.

Brassicas:

Try *Primo* and *Savoy King* cabbages. Or *Celtic, Stonehead,* or *Golden Acre. Greyhound* or *Spitfire* or *Hispi* for spring cabbage. There are a range of seeds suitable for round the year sowings. Personally, I wouldn't get involved with complex sowing patterns until you've found your feet.

For broccoli, dear old *Purple Sprouting* is fine. For calabrese (another sort of broccoli) try *Green Sprouting.* For something really exotic, you can't surpass *Romanesco.* It is a truly astonishing (and tasty) plant, and of remarkable appearance. I won't spoil the surprise for you here.

For kale, simple *Curly* does the business; go for the cheapest variety. *Ragged Jack,* if you can find it, is splendid. Non-obsessively-curly kales like *R Jack* are easier to wash clean than *Curly,* should aphids strike.

Try *Early Half Tall* for sprouts.

Roots, etc:

Autumn King is still one of the best carrots. Try it, along with a *Nantes* variety.

Parsnip... *Tender and True* is an old favourite.

Beetroot: *Detroit* is an old ball type, as is *Boltardy. Cook's Delight* is another old favourite, sweet enough to be eaten raw. Tell the kids it's Dragon Heart, dripping with gore.... *Cylindra* is more... cylindrical.

You really must grow some chard. The simplest, *Swiss,* is unbeatable, I think. *Perpetual Spinach* may be worth a try too. There has been a recent fashion for *Pak choi.* We grew it and it wasn't a patch on *Swiss chard.* You may find differently, of course.

There are fancy chards available, like *Rainbow* or *Ruby,* which don't crop quite as well as *Swiss. Ruby* however is of a quite frightening aortic arterial colour: very suitable for young boys to grow, if you see what I mean. They can tell all their friends 'You have to feed it on... blood.'

Speaking of colour... if you have the room and fancy a bit of fun, you might like to try a couple of 'fireworks'. *Ruby chard* is the obvious one. You can also get purple sprouts, yellow (or purple or white) carrots, red onions, yellow tomatoes and courgettes, purple or yellow climbing French beans, orange beetroot... no doubt someone is close to breeding a perfect blue and pink paisley patterned potato as I write. All good fun, and great for encouraging kids to eat healthy food.

For onions, try *Bedfordshire Champion*, *Sturon*, or *Ailsa Craig*. I would start with 'sets' if you can get them. Most garden centres etc will have sets. Try growing from seed next year to compare with the sets.

Musselburgh is the commonest old leek and works well.

All Green Bush is an old friend in the courgette world.

Salad crops means mainly lettuce, radish, tomatoes and spring onions.

For spring onions... *White Lisbon* still takes some beating. Very good for multi-sowing in cells, to be picked as instant bunches later on.

Radish: *Cherry Belle* and *French Breakfast*. (The French really *are* different, aren't they?)

Lettuce: *All the Year Round*; *Tom Thumb*; *Little Gem*; and above all, *Webb's Wonderful*. *Valdor* and *Winter Density* cope better than most with cold and wet conditions. If you can afford only the one sort, go for the *Webb's* or *Little Gem*. *Little Gem* is king for quick turnover and crispy leaves.

Incidentally, lettuce contains a mild soporific in its juices. If you have a sleep problem, try a couple of crispy lettuce leaves, and see what happens. If your partner's ears prick up and his nose starts to twitch, you're in trouble.

And finally sweetcorn: *Kelvedon Glory* is almost a trad variety, although it's only been for the last couple of decades that suitable varieties for GB have been available at all. *KG* is an F1, which means you'll get a glut, but I've never heard anyone complain of this yet. And anyway, you can freeze the surplus if you really can't force just one more down.

And really finally... can you find a perpetual corner for a bit of rhubarb? If so, try *Glaskin's Perpetual* or *Champagne*. Rhubarb needs good feeding, but is a very welcome spring fruit... if it is a fruit? Yes, it's a fruit in my book, anyway.

And speaking of perpetual corners... what about a few herbs?

Herbs are usually grown on a permanent patch, and cope with most soil types. Mints (pepper-, spear-, and apple-) are all a must, I would say. There are others. They all spread like crazy, so find a way of restricting their roots (a rusted-through bucket?). Lemon balm... fennel...dill... marjoram... nasturtium... sorrel... sage... rosemary... tarragon... and of course, chives, and Welsh onions. Egyptian onions are worth looking out for just for the fun of them. Be surprised! There's plenty of specialised information available on growing herbs. Personally, I'd just bung a few in and see how they do, *then* read the experts' views. Don't forget lavender for its decorative value and aroma, and for making up sachets to keep clothes moths off your undies (while in storage, of course).

And of course, basil. Grow this fresh, as an annual (read the seed packet). Try it with your own toms, sliced in a salad or on an open sandwich, or perhaps as a fresh home-made pesto sauce. You'll never buy anything as delicious. Very roughly, in order of quantity: basil leaf and posh olive oil (about half the total weight between them), with a touch of parmesan, garlic, and salt; plus a few pine nuts. Whizz them. Drool. Fight off the rest of the family.

Vary to taste.

Tomatoes in the next chapter.

This list is pretty rudimentary, but it's meant to be just a starter. Any decent seed catalogue will help with more detail. I recommend one such in Chapter 19.

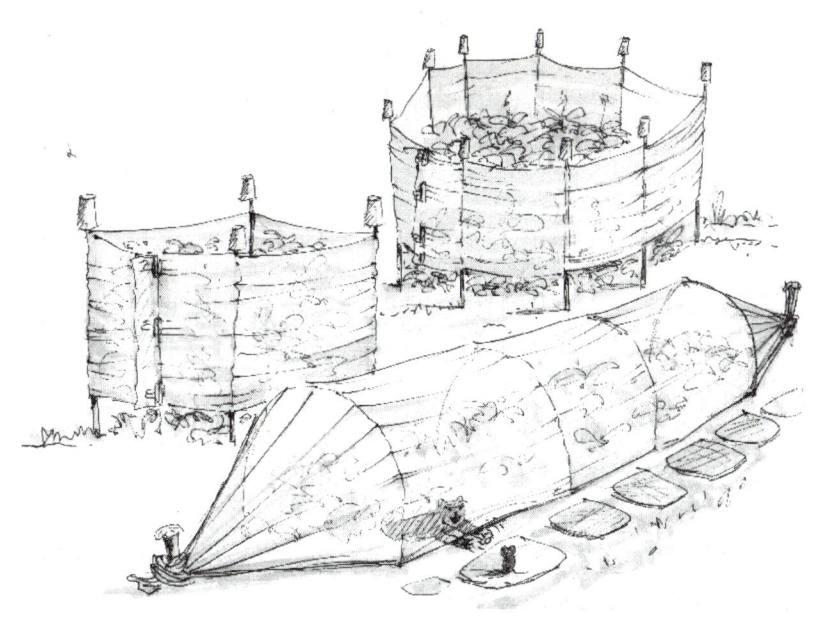

chapter 13
Protection

The British climate being what it is, it's no surprise that a lot of the plants we can grow here welcome a bit of protection, especially in their early weeks: just like children; just like puppies.

What they mainly need protection from is frost, which destroys their leaf structure; deluge, which literally drowns their roots; and wind, which withers and starves them. Hence, most gardeners try to provide some sort of help. Beginners tend to think in terms of expensive heated greenhouses, but you really don't need such things, unless you are determined to grow pineapples in Inverness. Good luck.

As ever, it pays to think things through before rushing out and wasting money.

What does protection do? It keeps out the cold (wind and rain), and keeps in the warmth. So far, so obvious. But it must also allow in a controlled amount of fresh air, and as much light as possible. People rarely pay any attention to what a miracle a plant is. From within its own starchy little seed it produces an entire inter-linked system of solar panels, and the structure upon which these panels can be efficiently distributed. It also produces roots which go down to trawl the moist, and hopefully nutrient-rich, earth. Within the solar panels it sets up an amazingly intricate system whereby it converts carbon dioxide and water into the dozens of different aspects of its own body, plus totally different systems like flowers, tubers, fruits and seeds of all kinds, which will, in the following season, each be able to reproduce this astonishing catalogue of feats. And all this is reproduced countless trillions of times a day, by creatures which apparently have no brain or mind. A miracle so commonplace that almost everyone fails to notice it.

To do all these stunningly complex tasks a plant must have light, and plenty of it. So... all you need is something that keeps the weather out and lets air and light in. (It makes you wonder what 'light' really *is*, doesn't it?)

Next... what do you want to use the protection for? There are seven main reasons for protecting plants:

1   To enable you to grow exotica like aubergines and melons that would struggle badly outside.

2   To increase the odds in favour of plants that *can* make it outside, like tomatoes and squashes.

These are the obvious uses. Also, and again obvious...

3   To develop and protect seedlings. Sow your seed into pots or cells or directly into the ground under some sort of protection, and they are going to have a much better chance of making it through infancy.

A little less obviously...

4   To enable an energy boost to ordinary crops like lettuce, potatoes, beetroot... almost anything that grows outside will enjoy growing inside, and will crop more quickly.

5   Following on from 4: to extend your growing season. With protection, you can have a picking of French beans a week or more earlier than usual; a couple of early spuds will give you a super-early treat; your strawberries will be ready for Wimbledon. And it's the same at the end of the season: a courgette plant will crop on for another week or two; *Swiss chard* never seems to stop.

      If you get really keen, you can buy special varieties of certain plants that will continue to grow and develop all through the winter. We once had dozens of enormous tasty lettuces for sale in *April* when most other people's plants were just a couple of inches high, or still unsown.

6   Drying and maturing crops like onions and garlic, or for more exotic treatments like making your own sun-dried tomatoes and apple rings.

7   'Hardening off'. Unless you're Swedish, or mad, or both, you wouldn't expect to run stark naked from a heated room into a freezing one, would you? It's the same with plants. They need a little time to adjust. So, if you've raised some seeds on a warm windowsill, or in a propagator (see below) it's vital to let them adjust to the great outdoors slowly. An unheated greenhouse, or cold frame or anything similar will do fine. Give them a couple of days in there, then plant out.

I suppose you also might add:

8   Keeping pigeons, rabbits, mice, voles, crows, cats, dogs and elephants off your precious crops... at least for a while. Also, if you get it right, white butterflies, aphids, weevils, and maybe some slugs, moulds and fungi. However, you might also keep out beneficial pollinating or predatory insects, and the crops do need a current of air, so you can't just lock

your protection down tight. Stay alert, and adjust things as you think fit. Netting makes good protection against lots of things while letting all the air through. Food production, like democracy, requires constant vigilance. Well... *fairly* constant. For heaven's sake don't obsess about it. Enjoy it!

We've grown everything you can think of, from carrots to grapes, in our two polytunnels. For a couple of years one of them was devoted totally to radishes, of all things. The protection meant they would grow at a regulatable pace, unchecked by drought or deluge, watered regularly, and could be harvested literally by the fistful, for washing and packing.

'Control' is the key word: very handy in an unreliable climate like the UK's, so, if at all possible, you really should organise some sort of protection, even if it's only a little. It's just so *useful*.

As an organic person, you are naturally concerned about global warming, and understand that every newly fabricated object causes CO_2 to be released into the atmosphere, along with more directly noxious fumes and poisonous effluents. Thus you will be keen on the three 'R's': **R**educe, **R**euse and **R**ecycle. And thus, you will be keen to scavenge whatever you can that will do the job. Skips and rubbish tips are an organic gardener's treasure trove, especially as a source of old windows. Use your ingenuity to convert them into useable protection.

Pale plastic bags have their uses for cutting down on wind and trapping a bit of warmth. Even dark ones can come in handy for frost-proofing individual plants overnight.

Don't forget that old plastic pop bottles are invaluable as individual cloches. (A cloche is any sort of protection which is applied directly over the plant. The name derives from the French word 'cloche'(!) meaning 'bell', referring to the old and beautiful glass bell-shaped jars that were the first... cloches. Gosh, that was hard work, wasn't it?) Of course, you can cut the bottle in half and you'll have two shorter cloches. Make sure air can move in and out, perhaps via a few holes burned through with a hot bodkin or little screwdriver.

Bubble wrap is brilliant, too. I know I've said this before, but some truths are worth repeating. Pester every trader in the district, particularly vendors of white goods, to save you all his waste. It's a nuisance to him, and he'll be delighted to give you bales of it.

Plastic sheeting is good, of course. But make sure it's ultraviolet-proof. Builder's polythene is no good as the sunlight will soon denature it and it will crack up into millions of irritating flakes of horticultural dandruff which will blow everywhere. Your neighbours will hate you, and quite right too.

Invest in bamboos to use as poles to thread, wrap, glue, tie, staple, gaffer-tape or rivet the sheeting to. Ordinary bamboo lasts for years and is cheaper and better than the fancy green sticks they sell in garden centres.

Scavenge bricks and broken blocks with which to build the base of a rudimentary cold frame.

If you'd like to move up the scale, you could make a taller cold frame, with glass sides and an easily openable lid, suitable for quite tall plants in pots. You can buy these, often under the name of an 'access box'. They may be pricy, but they look nice and are often well made. Don't buy tacky. Stick with home-made until, and if, you want a proper one. All garden equipment takes a proper pasting from the weather and ultraviolet sun rays. Prefer aluminium to plastic every time.

Higher yet, and you have the greenhouse in a hundred different varieties, ranging from a length of plastic sheeting nailed onto a wall with a batten, then dragged out and buried, to give a little triangular walk-in lean-to, right up to wrought iron confections like those magnificent Victorian orangeries.

If made of sturdy stuff, simple DIY jobs can work well, especially if insulated with bubble wrap, but they do need to be built much stronger than you might think. One single gale... We once had a bit of a blow one night that blew all the doors out of our polytunnels. Most of them we tracked down the next morning in a neighbouring field, but one of them, a 6' x 4' frame, covered in polythene, we never saw again.

If you decide on a greenhouse, do your homework. A lot of small ones seem to me to be an expensive luxury, with barely enough room to swing a cat (which shouldn't be in there in the first place, unless locked in to catch the occasional mouse who will love all the free seeds he finds there.) Will you get your money back at the rate of a few pounds of tomatoes every year? But maybe it's the allure of decent proper *tasty* toms that drives you on. Fine. It's money better spent than on an oversized tv.

At the top of the tree, and if you can afford it and have the room I would definitely recommend a polytunnel. There are all manner of shapes and sizes available these days. They tend to be much cheaper than glasshouses, but of course, the plastic will need to be replaced every few years as weak spots develop, usually by rubbing and eventually tearing at points of contact with the framework. The good news is that much of this plastic will still give good service as 'tube cloches' (see diagram and Chapter 8) or maybe as short 'tunnel cloches'.

A 'tunnel cloche' (see drawing at the front of this chapter) is a great way of protecting a couple of rows, or if you think it through, a whole bed of seedling plants. All you need are wire hoops, easily home-made from a bale of fencing wire, and a suitable length and width of uPVC plastic (the 'u' means it's proofed against the ultraviolet sunrays). The trick is to get the plastic taut enough to keep it from ripping itself apart on a windy night, but also loose enough so that you can lift it a bit here and there to let air flow. There are many commercial varieties to try. Maybe you'll prefer to try a commercial version first, before using your own creative ingenuity to make better ones, cheaper. Don't forget that flimsy plastic is a false economy.

You may have strong views on using plastic at all. Personally, I don't have a problem with it, as long as you use proper durable stuff that will last for years. It's much better used for growing healthy food than for pointless children's toys that either fall apart in a week, or crack into dangerous shards after a year of sunlight on them. Most plastics never properly decompose. They just break up into ever smaller pieces. Not even the great mill of the sea can decompose plastics. It merely grinds them ever finer. Every ocean fish you eat will almost certainly have scores if not thousands of tiny grains of plastic in it.

Another 'warming' use for plastic is to lay down black uPVC over a bed a week or two before you plant into it. The 'black' absorbs warmth and transfers it to the soil. You then cut suitable holes or slits into the plastic and plant through them. The black will continue to add a bit of stimulating warmth. Courgettes planted like this will crop at least a week earlier than when planted into bare earth. A word of caution: if anything gets inside the plastic, it'll never get out again. We've had voles running up and down a 200foot long bed, pushing up the plastic with their backs as they galloped along their little furry motorways, all nice and warm and dry, and we couldn't do a thing about it. Thank heavens we don't have pythons round here. This plastic is removed every winter and is re-used for many years.

Other interesting materials are perforated plastic, and 'fleece'. They both do much the same job, acting as a sort of broad low-level cloche to protect a patch of seedlings. You plant out your plants, than drape the fleece over them, and tuck the sides into the ground. No hospital corners, obviously, or the plants will be squeezed flat. It's all soft and gentle stuff. We always found that using stones to weigh the edges down, instead of digging them in, worked fine.

The idea is that the fleece, by its all-embracing nature, will keep pests off, and, being semi-permeable (it's a loosely-woven fabric) will let rain through. It lets plenty of light through, too, and acts as a heat-retaining cloche as well. Leave it on until you judge that the plants are strong enough to cope. For example, a bed of brassica seedlings can be destroyed in an hour by a couple of pigeons, but once they've grown a few inches tall, they will probably withstand a casual pigeon visitation, if not a determined assault by flapping hordes. Just keep easing the tension in the fleece as the plants grow.

It is also a good protection against frost, at any time. Just nip out with the fleece, drape it over your vulnerable plants, make sure it can't blow away, and there you are.

A length of fleece should last for many years. I'm not sure if the perforated plastic would be quite as tough. Personal judgement time.

Maybe a propagator would be useful? This is really just a seed tray to put soil or compost in, with a neatly-fitting plastic lid with ventilation holes in, and some form of heating system. This is usually an electrical under-soil wire. Useful for plants that need a long growing season, or which are very slow to germinate, and of which you only want two or three specimens of each. Peppers, aubergines... trials of new varieties...

That's about it for 'protection'. It's all common sense, really. A seed *will* germinate, given the chance. If it has come from exotic climes, it will welcome a bit of help in the form of a bit of warmth. Once established, it may then grow fine outdoors, or, more likely, it will benefit greatly from protection from our erratic weather throughout its life.

What to grow?

Tomatoes are top choice. Most types *will* grow outdoors, but will grow better under protection. Check on the seed packet.

Trad varieties include *Harbinger*, *Alicante* and *Ailsa Craig*. *Golden Sunrise* is a lovely cheerful yellow type. For 'cherry' types, try *Gardener's Delight*. For enormous 'beef' types, *Marmande* and *Beefsteak* are good. For Italian 'plum' types, as used in the canning industry, *Roma*.

Some of these may be harder to find than others. Don't worry about it. Try something else if you think it might suit, but do avoid 'F1' varieties unless you want 50kg of fruit all ripening at 3pm one day.

Most toms grow like lianas... up and away, and need staking with bamboos. You might want to pinch out the top 'growing point' when the plant has got as high as you want it to. It will also send out shoots from the joint between the stem and the leaf (I like to think of this development as the equivalent of armpit hair). Pinch these out, too, or too much energy will be diverted into them instead of into the fruit.

Some toms are bushy in shape (check the seed packet). Personally, I find bushy jobs easier to cope with, if growing them outdoors. *Marmande* (see above) is bushy, and seems to cope well outdoors too.

Cucumbers are next on the list. Cukes can be tricky, we've always found, as they tend to 'dampen off', which means they shrivel at the base and expire. This is apparently because we aren't watering them properly, though I can't see what we've been doing so wrong. Some always survive, though.

Try growing some from seed and buying in a couple of others as sturdy seedlings. (Don't bother with feeble floppy chemically-addicted things.) That way you give yourself a double chance of getting some right.

I'd recommend getting an all-female type. These are all F1's which means you'd better be keen on cukes. There are now mini-cuke varieties which produce lots of shorter fruits.

If you go for a trad type, *Telegraph* is the one. This is a normal male-and-female plant. You should pinch off any male flowers as soon as they appear, as fertilised cukes can be too bitter to enjoy. Male flowers are the ones with no tiny little cuke behind them. You need to be alert to catch them all.

On balance, I reckon you'd be best off going for a trad outdoor type (called 'ridge cucumbers') to start with, of which the aromatically named *Burpless* is top choice. Perfectly good cukes without the hassle. They're just a bit less smooth and erotic-looking, unless you know something I don't know.

If you have the room, you might try a squash or two, but be warned, once they get moving they can run faster than you can. 'Feed me!' The *Butternut* you grow yourself will taste better than the shop ones. Personally, I prefer *Buttercup*, if you can find it. It looks like a large green pork pie and is quite delicious; a bit like roasted chestnut. There are lots of astonishingly shaped squashes around to experiment with. Don't get too carried away too soon! Softly, softly...

Melons: try *Blenheim Orange* as a trad type or *Sweetheart* as an F1. Who cares if you have twenty melons to eat all at once? Melons can be tricky as they need a steady warm temperature. But they are definitely worth a try.

Strawberries: there seem to be new varieties coming out every other week. I would suggest asking around and seeing if you can get a few little plants for free from somewhere. Strawberries send out shoots which loop over the soil and then take root when they touch. Fantastic, eh? Just another miracle. These little off-shoots are called 'runners'. Other gardeners are usually keen to dig up and pass on their runners to someone who can use them, especially if the alternative is to just compost them. See how their freebies do for you before lashing out on a particular variety. Strawbs can be a bit difficult to hang on to. Everything in the natural world seems to fancy them, from voles and slugs to a fair array of moulds and mildews. Cloches are a good idea, but be sure of good ventilation.

You might also like to consider making a strawberry barrel one day. Basically, this is an old barrel, or similar (an old Burco boiler, or a damaged rain barrel? Maybe a cracked 3 gallon bucket?) with holes knocked into it, painted blue to show off the reds and greens of the plants, filled with rich soil (meaning, of course, 'with plenty of compost') and strawb plants stuffed into the holes. You will thus have made a pretty garden ornament that earns its keep. Ideal for a child to take on as a tasty responsibility.

There's more to it than this, but this small book doesn't have room for fine detail. (See Chapter 19 for a brief reading list).

Clearly, protection of the sort you can walk into (as opposed to variations on the cloche) is best suited for genuine exotica like aubergines (*Black Beauty*, *Long Purple*), peppers (*Bell Boy*), chillies (*Flaming Bowel of Satan's Wrath*... no, I just made that up; no proper recommendation here), and okra, if you like it (*Clemson's*), but I wouldn't rush into these species, especially not in the first year. The okra flowers are truly spectacular, though, so do try them one day.

Garlic definitely appreciates protection and takes up little room. Buy it as approved 'seed' rather than planting dried-out leftovers from *CrappoDeliBargains*. Stuff imported from Italy or Spain is unlikely to thrive in dank old Britain. Cloves sold in the UK as 'seed' are likely to have been bred in more northerly climes, like Brittany or the Isle of Wight, and will hence be more suitable. As a rule of thumb, we have found that the oval pink-skinned bulbs give cloves which grow much better in Wales than the round white ones.

***

A final thought on 'protection': if you are likely to have wind problems, you could do worse than plant a row of Jerusalem artichokes along the windy edge of your plot. These are actually relatives of the sunflower, and sometimes produce little yellow flowers to prove it. Under the ground they produce roughly potato-sized tubers which have a flavour of their own. Delicious with tomatoes as a soup. Wonderful baked. Just lovely stuff.

The reason I'm mentioning them here is that they grow several feet high and thus provide a creative leafy windbreak. Plant a double row perhaps, for extra protection and more soup. Remember that they will cast a shadow, so be sure you don't plant anything that needs plenty of sun too close to them. Tomatoes etc, need bright sun. Do a few experiments...

At the end of the year dig the roots up and harvest the tubers. You won't get a huge number of them, but no other windbreak will give you a better crop. Just re-plant one moderate tuber per plant for next year. Actually, you'll probably get more next year anyway, as they are notoriously elusive to harvest. A few always get away...

The dead stems are weak and not much use for anything, except smashing up and slowly composting, but I bet you could steeple a bunch together and grow a few climbing French beans or sweet peas up them. I've never tried it, but maybe you will?

Chapter 14
Storage

Obviously, you will have planned how much of what you want to grow in a season, and God willing, many of your crops will have survived the course. Some will be terrific; others moderate; and some will no doubt be dead losses. Don't worry... that's perfectly normal. Keep taking notes and observing every plant, thinking if there's anything you can do to improve the poor-performing crops. Might you improve on their watering regime? Did they get checked by a frost? Were they being over-shaded perhaps? I do recommend using your own common sense before rushing to books by experts. (More on books in Chapter 19). Think first and check later. It will help your self-confidence no end.

You know what seeds and plants need in order to grow: light, moderate water, warmth... and nutrients for the roots. That's about it. Even bare roots bathed in a chemical liquor will produce fruit of a sort. This technique is called hydroponics and is widely used for pepper and tomato production in Spain. That's why your *CrappoInc* out-of-season toms taste mainly of water. So do many of their in-season ones, because they were probably produced hydroponically too.

If your plants have been kept moist, and the weather hasn't been too ghastly, then you should get a crop. If you don't, then common sense suggests that the problem lies with nutrition. Vow to make extra compost, somehow. Make friends with the local Heavy Horse Artillery if necessary. Or a polo club. Or 'Trotties for Totties'. Anything... Maybe the Council has a composting scheme and could let you have a load?

Healthy soil is an immensely complex organism, and is largely self-balancing if you can just provide enough variety for the microlife to guzzle on.

You'll often see 'acidity' quoted as a soil problem. Well, yes, no doubt it can be, but speaking from personal experience, our soil is well below the 'ideal' level for growing courgettes, yet we produce top grade fruits at twice the rate the Man from the Ministry agricultural expert said we ever possibly could, even if our acidity was 'perfectly' balanced.

Don't *worry* about acidity and all the other 'techie' stuff. Just add some ground limestone powder to your legume patch every year. And don't worry about 'how much?' Common sense... Should you scatter it like fairy dust, in teensy little waftings, a pinch at a time? Or shovel it on a foot thick? Clearly, you should scatter it by the handful, thick enough to see its presence on the surface, but not to smother it. Being rock dust, it will release its calcium slowly, so it's most unlikely to ever cause an overdose problem, even if you get the 'correct' dose wrong by a factor of five.

It might be a smart idea to scatter it in the autumn, so the winter rains will have a chance to wash some of the calcium out and into the soil, rather than put it on in the spring and then promptly bury it by digging. But you'd already seen that one coming, hadn't you?

Or, you could scatter it over the rough spring digging, ready for it to be raked and scratched in to the soil more intimately as you prepare your seedbeds. Ahead of me on that one too, I expect. Excellent.

The other obstacle to a perfect 100% crop is pests and diseases, of course. We'll take a brief nod in their direction in Chapter 15.

Meanwhile, it's obviously not wise to store damaged goods. They will rot, and will take others with them. Your sack of hard-earned tatties may turn into a slew of evil-smelling gloop over a couple of months if you've not been properly vigilant when packing. It's a good idea to check them over once in a while, just in case one bad one has slipped through the net. No, I'm not going to define 'once in a while'. Use your judgement.

Roots and spuds need to have dried off before being loaded with moderate care into paper or hessian sacks. The skins are very thin, but remarkably mould resistant. Scratch them however, and they become vulnerable. It's the same with people, of course. We have more in common with plants than we usually think.

Trim the leaves off carrots, parsnips and beet, and give them time to heal the cut over before storing. You may prefer to twist the beet's leaves off, as this reduces the chance of the root 'bleeding'. Experiment. If you're feeling rich, you might want to make up a 'peat box' in which to store beet (or other roots). It's a box filled with peat, a layer at a time, covering the layers of roots as you place them within. Use the peat over and over, unless a crop rots in it, in which case chuck it into the compost and start again (on account of the rot having probably contaminated the peat). But you may have ecological objections to using peat, as the mining of it is said to release a lot of greenhouse gases.

You *can*, of course, leave the roots in the ground until you want them, but they are then open to assault by every hungry little critter in the district.

Check each root again as you pack it. Then close up the sack top in a light-tight manner, using either a bubble-pack of *Crappo Brand 100% European Sack Closure 'Natty-Knotties'*, or bits of a broken boot-lace.

Then store the sacks in a cool and frost-free place.

As the winter progresses, the roots will begin to stir. No, they will not start leaping about the shed at night, knocking all your tools off the wall and causing the local dogs to raise a howl, but they *will* send out little wispy rootlets and tiny shoots. From then on, it's a race against time for you. If necessary, break open the whole sack and cook/blanche and freeze the lot. Or gorge on them. Or give them away. Or force them down the cat. Or chuck them on the compost, and make a note to grow slightly fewer plants next year.

Swedes are normally just kept in nets, again, in cool, dry conditions.

Onions and garlic plait very nicely, if you want to keep some handy in the kitchen. Surpluses make wonderful and welcome gifts. They will also keep very well on trays or in nets in a cool place. If the onions begin to sprout before you've finished them, treat the green shoots as spring onions.

Brassicas are best left in the garden as long as they look healthy. Even ones that have clearly stopped growing and lose their outer leaves, will often have an edible heart within. If you have good hard-hearted specimens, you can cut and trim them in the autumn and hang them in nets.

Peas never get to the storing stage in my experience. If the dog doesn't get them, the kids will. Good.

Mainly, I expect you will have grown beans for their 'pods and all' value. But you might want to experiment with drying some for winter use. It's simplicity itself: just leave a few pods to grow on and then to dry on the vine. Eventually, the pod will desiccate completely and become papery and the beans within will be all but dry. Shell them out, dry them further, on trays in a greenhouse or on a windowsill. Then store them in a jar.

It's not a difficult job at all, but you may still not think it worth the effort, as dried beans can be bought very cheaply, and your garden space might be better used for growing vibrant green stuff.

Another drawback is that once a plant knows it has set seed, it begins to cut back on producing pods. How does it know? You tell me.

Leeks will hang on in the ground until you need them. People usually cut off and throw away the top foot or so of leek leaves. This seems to me to be a waste. Why not chop them finely, or drop them into the blender, and add to a soup?

You might like to experiment with tough outer cabbage leaves and carrot tops too. Beet leaves, of course... try them as a boiled veg.

Don't eat the leaves of potatoes though. They are poisonous, as are rhubarb leaves. And I expect tomato, pepper and chilli leaves are too, being of the potato family.

If you get busy in the autumn, your freezer will sustain you for a long period. We've found that the best way of storing a glut of courgettes is to fry up a few onions, then add tomatoes and the courgettes and cook-till-ready. Then divide into suitable batches in marge tubs and freeze. Instant ratatouille base for cold winter evenings. Add a few slices of potato for ratatattytouille.

The mix will also make a delicious base for a pasta sauce or soup.

That's about it for storing produce.

Now what about seeds?

Seeds are utterly astonishing little things: time capsules... messengers for the future... vectors of form. But they are also the means by which a species subtly modifies and develops according to the processes that lie behind the theory of evolution by natural selection.

The biblical parable of the seed-sower will illustrate how natural selection works very neatly. If seeds fall 'by the wayside' they are likely to be eaten by chickens; if they fall on stony places, with little earth and moisture, they get scorched; if they fall in a thorny area, the brambles will swamp them. Thus, the circumstances decide the future of each grain of seed. All the above would be 'selected out' and not get to breed. End of the line.

All very obvious. However, the principle that Darwin and Wallace realised was that not every single one of those disadvantaged seeds would die out. Soil is infinitely variable, from inch to inch. So, for example, one or two of the seeds that fell on stony places would have fallen into a niche that was slightly less stony, and might have struggled through for long enough to set seed after all. These new seeds would fall very locally, and would thus have also fallen on stony soil, and most would eventually die where they fell, but (and this is the super-astonishing bit) not all seeds are identical. In fact, no two 'natural' seeds *are* identical, any more than any two people or chickens are. Thus, some of the stony soil seeds would have been just a little more tolerant of drought than their siblings. They would be more likely to survive. And so on, down the generations, until the original species of, let's say barley, had now developed into a sub-species of 'drought-resistant barley'.

In the case of the seeds that fell among thorns, it might have been the individual seeds which grew slightly longer stems which survived. So another sub-species would eventually develop which could thrive amidst vigorous competition.

We now know that genes are involved in this process, and that it is genetic variation which defines these sub-species.

New seeds are formed when male pollen fuses with a female egg. Insects and the wind do most of the pollen carrying. I wonder if you've ever truly and deeply looked at a flower? *Into a flower?* I would guess that 99% of the population never have.

If you've missed out on this, get down on your knees one day and peer very closely at a common daisy or dandelion. If you have a magnifying lens, look closer. Unless you are certifiably insane, you will be astonished and maybe humbled at the unbelievable levels and complexity of design and structure in this commonest of little 'weeds'.

And next time you're in a garden (your own will be just fine) take time out to observe the activity within it. Watch a bumble bee at work. Get up close... she won't hurt you. See how the pollen sticks to her fur, and how she packs it into saddlebags on her legs. See how she works every little source of pollen in each plant. It's the pollen that sticks to her fur that fertilises the next plant of the same species that she visits. That tiny speck of yellow dust is rubbed off onto a sticky pad, and then *burrows its way down* to fuse into the waiting egg. The egg then begins (somehow, of its own accord) to develop and swell and turn eventually into a grain of wheat or a cabbage seed or an acorn, whose potential is released when the seed meets the right conditions. In terms of the parable, this is when the seed 'falls into good ground, and brings forth fruit, some an hundredfold, some sixtyfold, some thirtyfold.'

Ain't the whole process beyond belief? Yet it happens by the trillion every day.

Of course, and as a matter of passing interest, the biblical parable refers metaphorically to philosophical ideas or truths: sometimes these truths 'fall on stony ground' etc. The metaphor strongly suggests that human evolution follows a similar pattern to that of plants, except that what causes human evolution is mental development, not physical survival.

I find that very interesting, as it suggests that there is a higher dimension to 'evolution' than just fins and fur.*

To say that 'it's all genetics' doesn't actually explain the process of plant growth from seed to seed-producer, as genes are simply chemicals, with no mind or brain. Brainless chemicals cannot design the entire process whereby a seed spontaneously turns itself into leaves, stem, roots, and an incredibly sophisticated system of self-reproduction. Chemicals just ain't that clever. Unless you know otherwise, of course, in which case I look forward to you receiving your Nobel Prize!

But genes clearly do have a great effect upon the seeds which eventually result from sexual pollination, and this is of interest to gardeners who want to keep their own seed.

Strains and varieties remain 'true' by default, unless a freak 'sport' occurs. This sport is a genetic eccentric, which may, but probably won't, exhibit a desirable trait you can breed on from, if the sport is actually fertile, which it probably isn't.

You are on pretty safe ground if you choose to keep your own seed from anything but F1 plants. If you breed from these you will get F2 seeds, which will not breed true to type.** You might have a bit of fun with them though, just to see what turns up.

Another reason for starting with trad varieties is that you know they are suitable for seed-gathering.

Carrots, parsnips, beets (including *Swiss chard*) onions and leeks are 'biennial' plants, meaning that they spend their first year growing to size, and then storing up food in a swollen root or stem. In the second year they turn that stored food into producing seeds... unless we eat them in the meantime and pinch all their seed-food. What rotters we are.

So, if you'd like to keep your own carrot seed, say, let one chosen plant grow and grow. Pick one that looks strong in all senses. One day in its second year it will send up a remarkable shoot with umbrella-shaped groups of multiple tiny flowers. All sorts of little flies and insects will find nourishment in them, and will pollinate them as they go. By the end of the season the seeds will all have set and will be beginning to dry off. When you judge the time is right, cut off the whole stem one sunny day and put it head-down into a paper bag (rather than plastic... I'm sure you know why)*** and hang it somewhere warm and dry to finish off the drying process. Next spring, bang the stem about a bit and shake the seeds into the bag. Voilà. Lots of seeds. Maybe enough for your wants, even.

Bear in mind that if you are growing two different types of carrot and let them both go to seed, it's quite likely that they will cross-pollinate. It's probably best to avoid this complication until you are more au fait with the ways of Nature.

Any other biennial can be treated in much the same way. Use your common sense. The plant will want to produce masses of good seed. Your job is not to interfere too much and to collect them and store them in the dry.

Maybe one day you'll want to get more technical and actually lift your potential seed plants from the soil to be stored indoors out of harm's way over winter. You will then re-plant them in the spring, maybe in a pot under protection, and thus give them a real head start for the seeding season. But again, I wouldn't bother with this sort of thing just now.

Beans and legumes in general are 'annuals'. This means, unsurprisingly, that they grow, bulk up, and set seed all in the one year. Their energy mass lies within the seeds themselves... which we, rotters that we are, pinch.

Brassicas are not really worth saving seed from, as you may have trouble producing true seed. The point here is that all brassicas will inter-pollinate, including a few weeds like charlock, which will wreck your stock. If you do want to have a go, do it one species at a time, and be sure that none of your neighbours have let their kale or whatever bolt (go to seed) by neglect. To be on the safe side, you should check that nobody within a kilometre is doing this. Not really practicable...

You might persevere by putting a tube cloche round your plant, but insects will still bring alien pollen in.

The good news is that brassica seed is cheap.

We looked at spuds in Chapter 8. I would just repeat here that the tubers you pick for seed should be selected from the plants which are very good or good average. Don't go for extremes, or take all from just a couple of plants. Mix it. This is a sound rule for seed collecting in general, unless you are definitely trying to produce new varieties by careful cross-pollination and selection.

Lettuce is rather like carrot in the seed department, except that it is an annual. Pick one you like the look of, let it grow on and bolt. It will produce far more seed than you will need next year.

Tomatoes are easy. Pick a good fruit from your all-round best plant and let it over-ripen. Pick out the seeds, wash them if you like, and leave them to dry off thoroughly on a bit of newspaper. Beware of cross-pollination, of course, if you're growing more than one variety.

Radishes: let a good couple of examples bolt and let the pods dry off. Collect the seed, blah blah blah... you know the drill. If you're lucky, they won't have been pollinated by another brassica.

Anything else you fancy having a go at will fit one or another of these principles. It's all common sense, such as our ancestors used to have, but which has been wiped out of most of us by the 'expertisation' of our culture. And don't forget that most experts' opinions are likely to be only partially true at best, or hopeful guesswork at worst. What's for sure is that they will not be Holy Writ. What's more, no expert has seen your Plot and he thus doesn't know its quirks. You are your own best expert. Learn by watching, thinking, noting, and good old experience.

Soon you'll be wearing old tweed suits, smiling wry lopsided smiles and recalling for the benefit of a new gardener who has just bought you another pint, the summer of 2053 when we grew strawberries the size of melons. *That* big, they was...

It goes without saying that any plant you select for breeding should be the most perfect specimen (which does not necessarily mean 'the hugest', of course) you can find, even down to being less nibbled by caterpillars, as this may indicate that the plant is somehow slightly more resistant to this pest at least. Eugenics is alive and well in horticulture.

Finally... how long does seed keep for? This is another 'How long is a piece of string?' question, but it is a constantly niggling one. Very few people use every seed in every packet every year. Will you be able to use last year's seed this year?

You can try it and see, which could be time-wasting if they are duds. Or you could 'test sow' a few and see how they do on the windowsill or in the propagator. That's probably the most reliable way.

Broadly speaking, all seed should last for a couple of years after picking. The trouble is that although you might know when the seeds you have bought were packed, you don't know when they were *picked*, or how they've been stored.

If you have kept your seeds over winter in a cool, low humidity atmosphere (in closed tubs in the fridge is good) they will have a good chance of a good germination rate. Maybe you might sow a little more thickly, to pre-empt any duds? Of course, now and then they will come up at 99%, which means you're in for a bit of thinning out.

As a very broad rule of thumb... for seeds that were fresh when you bought them, which have been kept cool and dry over winter etc, etc...

Brassicas last for ~5 years
Courgettes ~5 years
Carrots ~4 years
Lettuce ~4 years
Onions and leeks ~3 years
Beans ~2 years
Tomatoes ~2 years
Potatoes... !

And surprisingly, parsnips tend to last only 1 year.

If you buy from an organic seedsman you can expect higher

quality seed, as organic people tend to be in the business on principle rather than purely to make money. Organically-grown seed is sometimes available, which will not have been in contact with chemical treatments. You choose.

Of course, your own seed will be the freshest. It will also gradually adapt to your own plot and local conditions if you choose carefully which plants to grow on from. Magic.

A final thought: if you're using the Square Metre idea, you might like to extend the experiment to taking seed from the plants on this patch. There's a certain attractive simplicity to this idea, it seems to me. Don't forget to stick with the sprit of 'rotation' on this patch.

* In fact I'm writing a book about this intriguing possibility, probably to be called *SuperEvolution: Darwin, Science, Religion and the Paranormal.*

** F1 seeds *are* very nearly identical but they are not entirely 'natural', having been carefully crossed for a specific reason. They are *not*, however, genetically engineered.

*** Just in case you don't... seeds that are drying off need to lose their moisture to the air, but plastic doesn't 'breathe' like paper does. Trapped moisture invites moulds and fungi. Yeuch. You could always try just leaving the seed-filled stem hanging bare, without the safety net of a bag. Good luck.

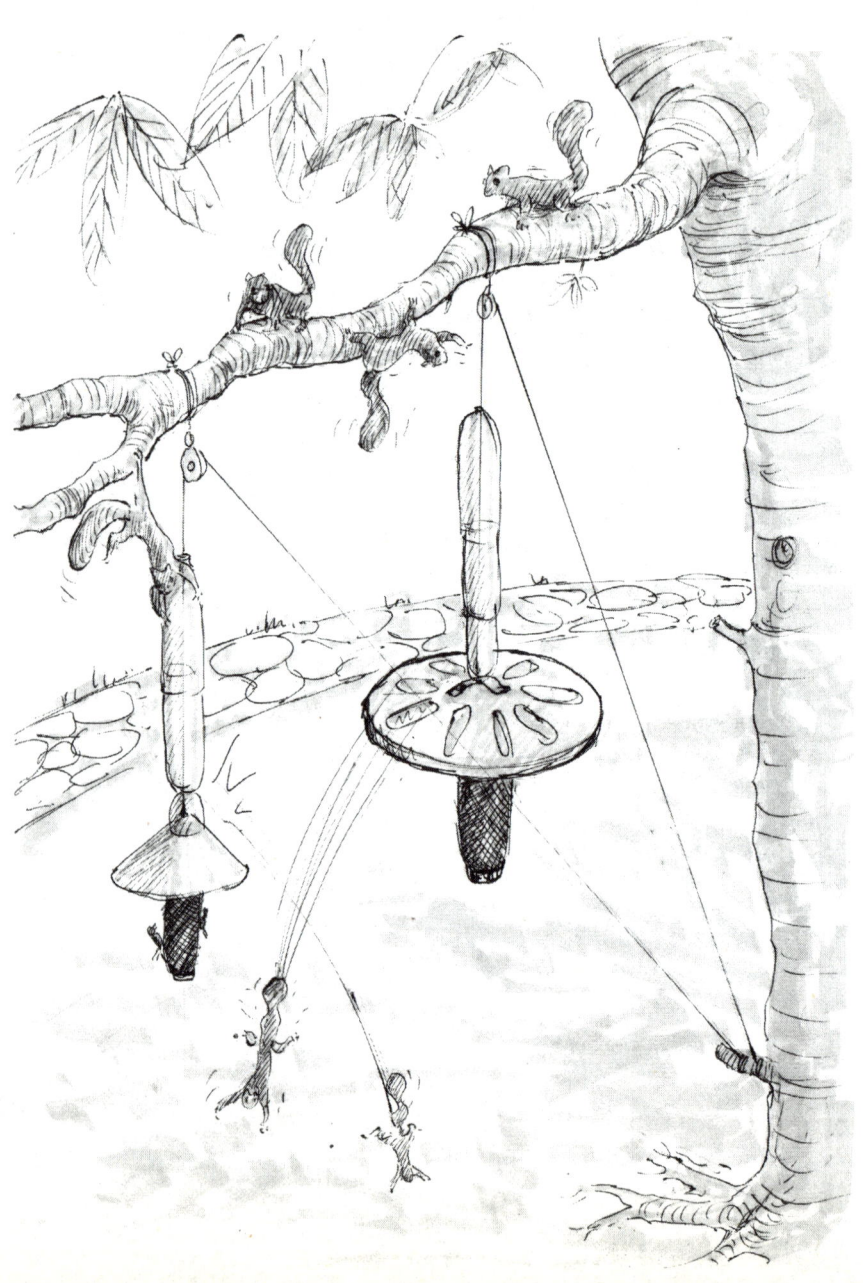

Chapter 15
Using your Head and Pests

I began this little book by saying that gardening is easy, because the only thing a seed wants to do is to grow. That is perfectly true. What makes gardening less than a hands-in-the-pockets doddle is the problem of *keeping* the plants, because every living creature needs to fuel itself and 'your' plants are often the best option around. Good enough for you; good enough for them.

If you are like me, you won't begrudge a carrot or two to carrot root fly, or even half a dozen lettuces to a rabbit. The problem is that they don't just eat one or two, they either *eat* the lot (rabbits) or *spoil* the lot (root flies).

For centuries gardeners and farmers have battled against spoliation, and the battle goes on today. By and large, farmers and most gardeners now use chemicals to kill pests in ever more intricate ways. Some sprays kill upon contact, by paralysis; others are systemic, meaning that the plant ingests the poison which then spreads throughout it: leaves, stem roots, the lot. Anything that eats it, dies. Others 'sterilise' the soil. Others are ingested from a surface and kill the animal from within.

It's a tough old business, keeping ahead of the pack, not least because insects and moulds and all the rest of the things that want to share our food have the astonishing evolutionary capability of adaptation, like the seeds that fell on stony ground and into thorns. Sooner or later, a strain of bug turns up which is immune to the farmer's sprays and the chemical companies then sell him something even more deadly... and at a suitably higher price. Who benefits?

Now the technicians are branching out into the minefields of genetic modification, with little thought for the implications for plant varieties in the future, as the genes in their chimeras escape into the wild... and your garden. 'Money *now*' is all that matters to them. That and 'If we can control the market so that you are forced to buy our modified seeds, you will then have to *keep* buying them from us, every year, because we'll make sure they are sterile so you can't breed from them yourself.' No... this isn't a paranoid fantasy. This is the deliberate policy of a cartel of multinational companies. Think of it their way: 'Control the seeds and you control the world's food. Control the food, and you can ask any price you like. Trillions or even quadrillions of lovely, lovely dollars! Possibly quintillions! Success!'

Two hundred thousand Indian farmers have already committed suicide as a direct result of having been unwittingly caught in this appalling and cynical trap. That's *two hundred thousand people* who have killed themselves because of the poverty trap they have been manipulated into by these seed/fertiliser/pesticide cartels; and the number is rising every year. This is part of the true cost of 'genetic modification' which, they tell us, is going to save the world from starvation. Quite the contrary say I, and many others like me.

Organic farmers and gardeners are more sensitive to the dangers of poisons, which are as likely to kill friends as foes. Ladybirds eat lots of aphids, and their curious purple and yellow crocodile-like infants do too. In fact, a single ladybird nymph will eat something like 400 greenfly aphids. One ladybird's offspring could eat 150,000 of the creatures in a single season. Valuable allies, not to be poisoned. If you *do* poison, the aphids which survive the spray (and some always do) can carry on chomping without concern, and will reproduce like the clappers. As a matter of interest, aphids are parthenogenetic, which means they can have babies without being fertilised... and at the rate of hundreds a week. I can't remember the precise numbers here, but someone once calculated that if all the offspring from a single aphid could all reproduce as they became mature, then over a single year they would cover the planet to a depth of several feet. This would be very inconvenient, so they must be checked. It is also a damn good thing cats do not have this gift, although sometimes I have my suspicions.*

But if you are wary of chemicals, how do you control pests?

What's the organic way?

As ever, it involves a lot of basic and lateral thinking, rather than following the tramlines of convention and orthodoxy. Let's take aphids... those little green or grey or black critters that suck the life-sap from your plants now and then; and as farmed by ants for their 'honeydew' exudations.

First of all, do you *need* to control your aphids? Have you actually got any? If so, are they actually a nuisance? Can you tolerate them? That's the easiest solution. If they aren't totally destroying your crop can you settle for sharing?

Next, what about your natural allies? Ladybirds, lacewings and hoverflies: read up a bit about these creatures (see Chapter 19) and learn to recognise them and their voracious larvae. Import a few if you see them pottering about in the park.

In the springtime, blue tits and similar small birds love pecking up aphids from their hidey-holes in cracks in tree bark. So if you hang up a column of peanuts (see cartoon for a ideas), the birds will turn up, and while they're waiting their turn on the nuts they'll fossick around in the locality for any tasty little bugs. Or hang a bit of fat up for them.

Check out which plants and trees the birds visit most. They're the ones that harbour the eternally-pregnant aphid-machines. Other will arrive from further afield of course, but maybe your own local aphid hotel could be (re)moved?

You could also do worse than to put up a couple of bird boxes to encourage tits and co to hang around. Get a free plan at: http://www.beautifulbritain.co.uk/htm/wildlife_gardening/ bird_box.htm

Next... there's a tropical tree called a quassia (say 'kwosha', if asked) whose wood or bark releases a very bitter substance when boiled up. This makes plants unpalatable to tiny critters. It's not a biocide as such, and should not thus be breaking any *Eurodiktat* if you use it. See what you can find on the net.

Next... a bit of lateral thinking. If aphids just love your lettuces, but are never seen on, say marigolds or rhubarb... well, there will be a reason for this. It might be that marigold juice is unpalatable. Therefore a spray made from marigolds might protect your lettuce. I've never tried this myself, but I certainly would if I was having big aphid trouble. Keep an eye open for other plants that are never troubled by aphids, and experiment. Chrysanthemum liquor?

Further down the list... soapy water. Apparently slightly soapy water will block the aphid's breathing apparatus. It's all to do with surface tension. I have used this, and it does work. Use soap rather than detergent. Experiment with dilution. Keep it as weak as possible.

Just when you thought it couldn't get any simpler: water. Get a little water-pistol, (not your *Cat-a-Pelt MogBlaster*, which would be too powerful for this job) and squirt the critters with it. It will have the same effect as a water cannon on the streets of Paris. Or just try an ordinary squeezy bottle.

And right at the bottom of the ingenuity list: a stiff paint brush. Lean the plant over. Whizz up. Whizz down. Bugs gone. Done. By the time you've driven to the garden centre, bought your expensive nerve poison, driven back, read the terrifying instructions, found your rubber gloves and goggles, locked the dog and the children in the garage, mixed it all up in a well-ventilated area (being careful not to drink any), and delivered it.. you could have solved the problem twenty times over with your squeezy bottle or little brush. Whizz up; whizz down...
A brush won't kill the aphids much (if you see what I mean) but it will knock them off the plant and they ain't built for climbing back up it. Beetles will get them if they're on the ground anyway.

Obviously, not all of these techniques will be suitable for every crop. I can't really see the paintbrush being much use on a lettuce, for example. But a ladybird dropped into a plant would be sure to do the business... until it flew off, of course. A friend once brought us a hedgehog to help with our slug problem. It ran away, and can only have escaped by climbing a chicken wire fence. We all have our own agendas, even hedgehogs and ladybirds.

The point I'm trying to make here is that we should approach every pest problem with an open mind and as much creative imagination as possible. To my mind, it's a sign of poor moral fibre, a lack of social responsibility, and criminal laziness to reach for the nerve gas first. Try everything *else*, first, and then still don't reach for the nerve gas. Experiment instead. Seek, and create your own wisdom. For example, I bet greenfly don't much care for a stiff jigger of urine and orange zest; or a spray containing (sorry about this...) a spoonful of mashed up aphids. I've never tried these potions either (especially not on my lettuces) as we've never had much of an aphid problem at 550 feet up in the hills, but I bet it works on suitable crops. The urine, of course, contains nitrogen, which is a handy fertiliser. You could try bottling and selling it. *'NEW Two in One Aphideath-N'*. I bet you'd sell a million bottles a year.

At the end of the day, think of it this way: if you can't outwit a greenfly, there's something wrong with you.

***

The principles above apply to all other garden pests and critter problems, especially the principle of observation + lateral thinking. Chickens, as you know, eat grubs and so forth. Might you therefore buy in a couple of hens to follow you round while digging? Or would they just eat all the valuable worms? Or maybe, if you give the worms time to hide, the nasty grubs would still be lying around on the surface? So let the chickens loose in ten minutes' time?
You get the drift.

Speaking of grubs and worms and yucky things like that...
There's a rule of thumb which is worth bearing in mind: if it moves quickly, it's your friend; if it moves slowly, it isn't. Can you see the rationale behind this?
Anything that moves quickly is likely to be a hunter, which

needs to cover a lot of ground to find its lunch. What will a garden hunter be hunting? Critters that move more slowly than itself. Who moves slowly? Critters that eat vegetation, who have no need to travel any faster than it takes to find your potato or carrot. Then they dig in, unless our rapid predator grabs them first. Centipedes, little orange jobs with too many legs and twitchy whiskers, and beetles are friends. Millipedes, little black watch springs are not. Big grey grubs are not either. They are called 'leatherjackets' because they are very tough. They cut off the roots of plants. What's more, they are capable of giving incautious fingers a little nip.

Worms are your very best friends in the garden. They process the soil in their gut and turn it into the ideal growing medium. Keep your eye open for worms while you're digging, and try not to hurt them. Note how the population increases in proportion to the amount of compost you provide.

There is no room here to make a full list of all the bugs and diseases you might come across (see Chapter 19 for the next step), but maybe it's worth picking out a couple of common ones to think about.

Brassicas are prone to several pests, which include clubroot and cabbage root fly. They both wreck the root system. The clubroot fungus is often imported on bought-in seedlings. Thus... don't buy in seedlings unless you are certain of their provenance. The fungus likes to linger in the soil, hence the importance of rotating crops. If the fungus doesn't get fed for three years, it will be severely weakened, and may even die (but nothing is certain in biology). It's also important to make sure you clear out any 'cruciferous' weeds (which are related to brassicas and thus can carry the fungus). These weeds include charlock and shepherd's purse. If you don't yet know these plants, you will soon (see Chapter 19).

The root fly burrows down into the soil at the base of the cabbage stem and does its dirty deeds out of sight. An effective preventative is to cut out a few collars of large beer mat size from old vinyl flooring or roofing felt, for example, and to slip them round the stem of each plant, in firm contact with the ground. Thus you must make sure they can't flap about too much. I guess corrugated cardboard would work as well, as long as you can keep it flat.

You might also like to experiment with making up a brew of carrot tops or urine, garlic, chrysanthemum, pine needles, fennel, lavender, sage, mint, etc to spray round the base of the brassicas. Surely something of the sort will deter the fly? You know the drill.

The problem with any sort of spray is that its effectiveness wears off, particularly quickly after rain. Might it hang around a little longer if mixed with a little old chip oil?

The key to any of these DIY sprays is to go about it systematically, so you can be certain what has worked and what hasn't. I suggest spraying a couple of plants with x, a couple more with y and a couple with z. Then spray a few more with x, y and z. Observe closely... make clear notes. Don't give up. Try a few cocktails. Something will work...

The other eternal pest is the slug. I sometimes give talks to local gardening clubs and the first thing people ask is 'How do you cope with slugs?'

There are lots of ways, but none of them is perfect, because there are dozens of different kinds of slugs and, unlike most other creatures, there are varieties that are active in every month of the year.

Starting with the simplest defence: general hygiene. Tidy up any dead leaves or trash. Slugs like to hide under damp things. It will also help if you cut back any surrounding grassy or weedy patches. We once lost every single lettuce in a dozen rows, up to six feet down from the weedy headland. I ploughed the headland over, and re-planted the lettuces. We didn't lose a single one. So trim back any long grass nearby.

Develop the habit of dealing with any slug immediately you find it. What you do with it is up to you, but do it now. Also, deal with any slug eggs immediately. These lie in clusters and look like small shiny pearls. Lift them out of the soil and dump them somewhere else. Or give them to the chickens.

There are a number of modern folk recipes for dealing with slugs. People swear that cinders, or chopped hair, or salt do the job. Yes, they will no doubt work by providing an unpleasant physical barrier, but once they get wet, or blow around a bit, their value is gone. Worth a try, though.

Then there's the upturned grapefruit shell. This will work as it supplies a nice damp hutch to hide under. You need to be fond of grapefruit, though, if you are to make a real difference.

'Slug pubs' work, too. These are either costly or home-made devices for pouring beer into, which the slugs gorge on and then drown in, rather like Croydon on a Saturday night. They say milk works well, too. Devise your own 'trap'.

One of the problems with slugs is that they are incredibly hardy. I once went round a patch of veg, picking up every slug I could find, and dumping them into a bucket of water, sure that they would then drown. Next morning I took the lid off: no slugs. Surely they can't have all dissolved? Nope... all thirty or so of them had climbed from the bottom of the bucket, through a foot of water, to nestle cosily under the lid. 'Damp place', you see...

You can exploit this tendency by leaving boards and sheets of plastic lying around at night. In the morning you'll find a few slugs beneath. Banish them as you think fit.

Hens don't often go for slugs, but ducks do. But even ducks sometimes meet their match. I've witnessed a mallard almost choke on an enormous slug, one with a 'go-slower' orange stripe round its skirt, the size of a budget-pack éclair. But ducks do a fine job. We'll say no more about hedgehogs.

If you really are suffering a pestilence, or are finding your courgette seedlings lying flat on the ground, all a-withered, having been neatly chomped off at the base, you may need to get serious. Old-fashioned slug pellets (using metaldehyde) are dangerous to wildlife, and should be avoided. But there is a new type based on ferric phosphate which claims to be safe in this respect, and which has been given the seal of approval by *Organic Farmers and Growers*, one of the organic watchdogs.

There is also a cunning solution which involves spraying microscopic worms called nematodes onto the land. They kill slugs their own way (see Chapter 19).

And don't forget to experiment with a garlic spray.

Finally, there is the metallic approach: warm copper or cold steel. If you wrap sticky-backed copper tape round your plantpots, any approaching slug will be given an electric shock. No, you don't wire it into the mains; it's to do with a natural property of the materials. No use on the plot, though, as dust and rain will quickly interfere with the necessary cleanliness.

But if you're feeling adventurous, you might experiment with making special little solar-powered electric fences against slugs. No, I'm not joking. They would certainly not work perfectly (if at all) but all help is welcome against slugs.

The cold steel approach involves a razor blade on a stick.

We were once growing a couple of hundred Chinese cabbages in a field, and they were being reduced to lacework by little grey snot-blob slugs. You know the sort, I'm sure.

We could find no solution to this until we decided that we had to take drastic action. For a week, four of us went out every evening with our blades on sticks, and did not return to base until we had despatched a hundred slugs each. The last couple of evenings were long, but it did the trick.

A final word on slugs: if you have a polytunnel, slugs like living down the crack twixt plastic and soil. Dig em out. A *Swoe* is useful for this; ideal, actually.

It also helps to keep the soil surface dry. Try to keep the water close to the plants and away from the plastic.

There's no room to go into more here, but ingenious anti-pest solutions are being developed all the time. For example, you can buy sachets of dried bacilli which will do for caterpillars on brassicas.

And, would you believe it, some genius has discovered that white fly, the bane of some greenhouses, are attracted to a specific tone of orange. Thus, if you have a card of this colour, coat it in grease, and hang it in your greenhouse...

Try *Pests – How to Control them on Fruit and Vegetables* by Pauline Pears and Bob Sherman, two great experts in the field of organic controls.

There is still plenty of room for ingenious solutions. Can you supply some more yourself? Musical tones? Other shades of orange!? Cedar shavings (as used to keep clothes moths at bay)?

* No, I don't hate cats. But I do protest strongly at the destruction they wreak on our garden birds. And don't forget that 'no birds' equals 'more insects'. More insects means more pests. More pests means less good food. And we *need* that good food. If people just keep their cats indoors while the birds are about that would make a huge difference. Just let them out at night... they'd prefer that, anyway, don't you think? ...all that slinking and lurking? And the possibility of taking on a Worthy Opponent like a rat instead of a titchy little blue tit?

chapter 16
Using your Head and Weeds

Chemical gardeners regard weeds as enemies: malicious entities whose only will is to thwart the virtuous gardener. This is reflected in the adverts for weedkillers. Next time you see one, look at the message that is being delivered. It's all about anger and hate and paranoia.

Organic gardeners think differently, because they respect Nature, and want to work *with* it, rather than wanting to dominate it. They thus respect all of Nature's beings, which includes weeds.

So don't just curse your weeds. Instead, get down on your knees and examine them in situ. Pick them up and look closely at them. Each one is every much as great a miracle as your favourite melon or potato, and is worthy of our respect, if only for the fact that they are the plants who have best adapted to the jungle out there over the past million years or so. If Man should ever succeed in reducing this beautiful planet to a pile of smoking cinders, it will be the 'weeds' who will begin its regeneration, ready for another influx of chancers.

Just for the record, what is a weed? A weed is plant in the wrong place, as defined by you. Thus a rose in the spud patch is every bit as much a weed as a spud in a rose garden. Unless you decide otherwise, of course. You may well think that an immaculate rose garden looks the better for having a lusty *King Edward* or two to set it off. I would tend to agree.

But it's a fact that most weeds are simply a problem, in that they are competing for the nourishment, light, and water that our own crops need. Most of them have to go, particularly as they are likely to swamp out our own chicken-livered little plants completely. But do it with respect. 'Sorry, but you've got to go...' (If you think that sounds a bit weird, wait till you see the next chapter...)

Broadly speaking, weeds spread in two ways: by seed and by root. Some can do both, and incorporate a couple of extra tricks of their own. You'll soon learn which does what if you take time to get to know them, and treat them accordingly.

It's best to bodily remove all weeds, especially while your own plants are still young. But if you're short of time, just chop off any seed heads with a pair of scissors or shears or a well-aimed Bowie knife. Do this at any time before the seeds have properly ripened. If the seeds are still soft and squishy, you can compost them. If they're getting a bit firm, I wouldn't risk it. Our precious veg seeds may last only a couple of years, but weed seeds seem to last forever. Some have seeds designed to germinate after one year, with more the year after, and others at irregular intervals for ten or twenty years or more. I know a lotus isn't a weed, but a lotus seed found in an Egyptian tomb was recently germinated after a couple of thousand years. It's my bet that nettles and poppies can beat even that.

Speaking of poppies... they may be 'weeds', but I always give them a bit of room. So might you, I expect.

As you get to know your *Scarlet Pimpernel* from your *Tormentil* and your *Nigella* from your *Yarrow*, you may find that you want to leave a couple of each plant here and there to brighten the place up. You might also want to find out why you have certain weeds and not others. In other words, can your weeds tell you anything about your land? First of all, get a decent wildflower book (see Chapter 19), of which there are now many to choose from, and learn to identify every plant on your plot. This should be a fun thing to do. Some of them have come a long way to share your life. Nettles, for example, were brought over by the Romans. Nice old Romans.

Your book may give some indication of what soils the weeds/wildflowers prefer... which will be a clue to you. Nettles like nitrogenous soil, for example. This means that if you have thriving nettles, your soil must be pretty rich in 'N', which is the basis of the nutrient needed by leafy plants. Thus your nettle patch should be naturally good for cabbages.

Sorrel, *Creeping buttercup*, and *Mare's tail* all suggest that your Plot is on the acidic side. A dose of powdered limestone will help.

Sherlock Holmes would love this stuff.

What else...?

Reeds, not surprisingly, indicate poor drainage. This could mean that the roots of your plants will drown. If the land is clayey, you may be able to solve this by deep digging to break up a shiny, impermeable 'pan'. If you do deep dig, be sure not to bury your biologically active topsoil (the top 4-6 inches) under the inert subsoil you disturb. You can tell the difference by the colour. An alternative to all this labour is to dig a drainage tunnel. This is often more effective at the top of the patch rather than the bottom. Try both!

If you plant your crops as closely as reasonably possible, you will naturally tend to crowd weeds out, by literally taking up 'their' space with your own plants. You will judge how close is close. Let experience be your guide. If you plant over-closely, you may find that getting a hoe in is impossible, and you're spending all your time on your hands and knees, ripping out weeds with your teeth, which isn't the idea at all.

If the crop's foliage tends to spread out, this can be a bonus. Carrots and potatoes are good at this. Once they have really got away, one row's leaves meet the next row's leaves, and no normal weed can get enough light to germinate. Docks and thistles might force their way through, of course, because they have all that power in their roots to draw upon.

Any 'rooty' sort of weed needs more careful underground attention than a 'seedy' sort. When digging thistles, try to get as much of the root out as possible. Loosen the soil around the stem with your spade (or better, fork) and then slowly haul the stem up and out. When it resists, loosen the soil some more and gently haul again. *Creeping Thistle* has a wonderful survival system. If you don't get out every bit of cabling above about two millimetres thick, the remaining root will inevitably send up more shoots. It's worth a bit of patience, teasing it out. But, if you prefer, any rooty weed can be gradually killed off by consistent hoeing off of its shoots. No leaves means no light. No light means no growth. All the energy must thus come from the root, and you, you beast, keep chopping the new leaves off, thus exhausting the root.

You may like to consider flame weeding. This is not an Arnold Schwarzenegger operation. What flaming aims to do is to rapidly pass intense heat over a new seed bed, destroying the cells in a tiny leaf by boiling the water in them. This requires far less energy than the 'Die, asshole!' approach of incinerating everything to smouldering ashes.

Our farm equipment consists of a wand with a double burner and a trigger control connected by a rubber pipe to a big orange tub of propane. One of us delicately wafts the wand around, while the other hauls the big heavy canister uphill, one step at a backbreaking time. Yes, you've guessed who's on the canister end.

Flame weeding is most useful on beds with 'small seed' plants in them, like carrots. These are the ones most likely to be quickly swamped by weeds.

Here's the procedure:

Dig and rake your land. Knock it down some more until it's small enough to rake into drills for sowing small seed into.

Leave it for a few days... up to a week, or maybe a little longer if the weather's poor, then flame weed. The bed will appear at first glance to be almost totally bare, but if you look closely, you will see dozens of tiny little leaves *just* emerging. Now is the time to zap them, and to then sow your carrots. The carrots are now on an even footing with the next wave of weeds. Weeds, by definition, germinate faster than carrots, so you zap them again (and here's the tricky bit) just *before* the carrots emerge. This isn't as tricky a judgement as it sounds, actually. First of all, carrots take about ten days to emerge, give or take, depending on the variety and the weather. The weeds will be a day or two quicker. But it would be helpful to have a more reliable guide that this, wouldn't it? Any ideas?

Here's one: lay a piece of glass or suitable plastic across a couple of feet of a carrot row after you've sown them. The extra warmth will stimulate the seeds beneath it. After a week, check every day, and poke the soil gently beneath the glass. No doubt you'll find a lot of tiny weeds on their way, but also a few tiny carrots. They send out two pointed leaves from the very top of the stem, a recognisably bright carroty green. You'll soon recognise them.

To make sure you do, you could sow a pinch of four or five under one corner of the glass, and mark the spot with a twig or a pebble, or, if feeling particularly flamboyant, a rare sapphire of exquisite quality.

If these carrots have indeed germinated, you can be sure the weeds on the rest of the patch will be ready for zapping. Do it.

You literally just wave the wand across the patch, 2-3 inches above it: just enough to heat-wash the surface as you proceed at a slow walk. It takes no time at all, unless you're heaving a whopping great orange tub of explosives uphill, in which case it takes forever.

If you think flaming might be useful for you, equipment suitable for gardens is available. Or perhaps you could hire it? Or maybe the whole thing is just too much trouble, or the size of your plot doesn't merit it. It's a useful tool to know about though.

And it is extremely effective. Following the above procedure, we have had carrot beds completely free of weeds for a couple of weeks, bar the occasional smoking stump of an overlooked dock: plenty of time for the carrots to roar away, unchecked. Meanwhile, a small corner that we deliberately didn't flame was a hopeless mass of weeds, with nary a carrot to be seen, even after close examination. We abandoned it, re-dug it, and re-sowed. Then flamed it.

I guess this is the right place to discuss other weeding tools.

If you've got a proper slicing hoe, which will cut on the pull as well as the push, and which can be used at an angle to chivvy awkward specimens out of small cracks, then you really need very little else. Especially if you've got a decent sharp knife; a sheath knife does take some beating, but an ordinary table or carving knife can be good. Actually, you might like to try out some other cutlery, too. A Victorian fork, the sort with big long prongs, is handy for getting under the roots of small grass clumps close to an onion. A big spoon is worth trying out. It may also bring unexpected gifts. I was once scratching away at a patch of chickweed with a big silver-plated serving spoon when a passing cyclist stopped and offered me a half-eaten cheese sandwich and an apple core from his saddle-bag. The kindness of strangers.

I would definitely resist doing the consumerist thing of buying stacks and stacks of fancy tools 'as advertised on tv and in the press!!' You don't *need* the JML *WeedWorrier*™ to shake off the last bits of soil from your weeds to make them perfect for the compost, 'batteries included' or not.

Work with your basic tools for at least the first season, and get to know their capabilities. Just because something is called 'a rake' doesn't mean it can't be a weed worrier as well, or a bonfire prodder and feeder, or drill tamper, or stone shifter, or shell cracker. A rake can also be useful for perforating several holes in the sole of your wellington before rising up and smacking you across the nose. (Always leave rakes prongs-down.)

By all means buy in another tool later, when you're sure it will fill a definite gap in your armoury, but only buy it when you're absolutely sure. I had a friend who swore by his traditional onion hoe. This is a little swan-necked hand-tool, with a half-moon chopping blade, designed for hoeing round onions. I bought one at a boot sale, but quickly found it pointless. My *Swoe* was much better, and I'm sure the inventors of the onion hoe would have agreed with me if the *Swoe* had been available in Victorian times. Above all, *never* buy a carrot dibber, even if heavily advertised at a very attractive price.

One of the advantages of leaving the odd flowering weed about the place is that they will attract pollinating insects. You might like to go a step further and deliberately plant a few 'bee plants' or 'butterfly plants' (see Chapter 19).

You might even like to leave a nettle or two in a quiet corner, as they provide food for the small tortoiseshell butterfly, one of Nature's jewels, now under dire threat from pesticides and ruined habitat. It will be bound to become extinct if we continue to extend our present lunatic dependency on oil-based chemicals and our ruthless exploitation of every square foot of land to produce food that has a one in three chance of being simply thrown away. Farms which have backed off a bit, and left a corner or two to go wild, have seen a return of beneficial and beautiful insects, and pest-controlling birds. It can be done. Every organic farmer and gardener knows this, and does his bit.

While we're on the subject of unexpected plants, there is a lot of interesting experimentation to be done around 'companion planting'. There is a traditional belief that inter-planting carrots with onions keeps away the pests of both. Whether this works or not, I couldn't say. I've never tried it. But in theory at least, this is an idea worth pursuing. Anyone with a privet hedge knows that nothing else will grow close to it. Why not? Is it just too dry near the privet for anything else, or does the root give off a chemical of some sort? Come to think of it, I wonder if a spray made from privet clippings would be useful as a deterrent to some sort of pest?

One plant that definitely seems to have an effect is *Tagetes*. If planted in a greenhouse, it deters whitefly. There must be hundreds of such simple secrets waiting to be discovered. And who better to discover them than a creative gardener like yourself?

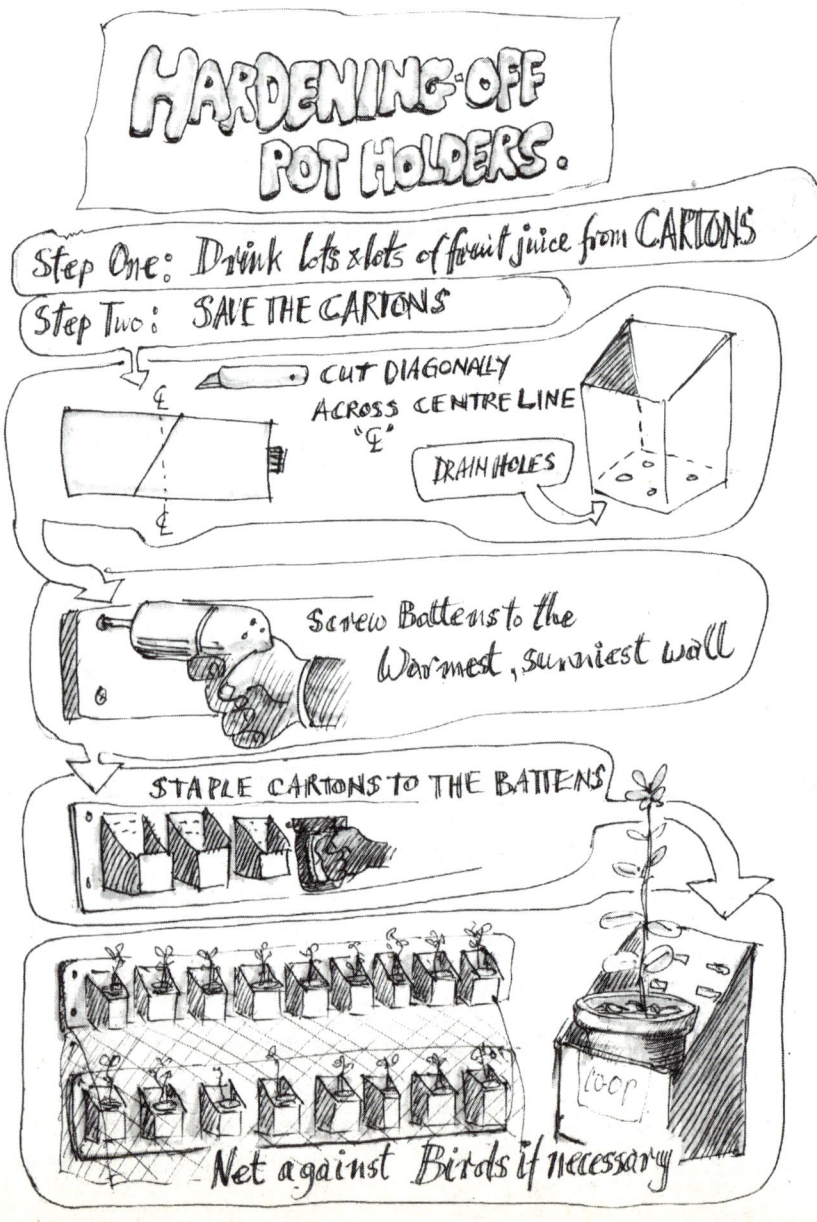

HARDENING-OFF POT HOLDERS.

Step One: Drink lots & lots of fruit juice from CARTONS

Step Two: SAVE THE CARTONS

CUT DIAGONALLY ACROSS CENTRE LINE "₵"

DRAIN HOLES

Screw Battens to the Warmest, sunniest wall

STAPLE CARTONS TO THE BATTENS

1000

Net against Birds if necessary

Chapter 17
Weirdo Stuff & a Few Tips

Tips first, mostly obvious...

Do modify your rotation if it suits you. Just keep the principles in mind.

Cells and pots may get 'pot bound' if the weather prevents you from planting them out bang on the button. 'Pot them on' (meaning 'transfer them to bigger pots with as little disturbance to the roots as possible') if you need to. Signs of pot-boundness include yellowing of leaves and simply not growing any more... (that 'constipated' look)...

...leading to this thought: a plant's only ambition in life is to set seed, to ensure the continuation of the species. If it feels stressed, it might panic and set fruit early, thinking its time is up. Cunning growers can use this knowledge to get earlier fruit. But beware... It's easy to accidentally kill the plant.

It's traditional to follow early spuds with leeks to make best use of an empty space. Would this suit you and your rotation?

If you have any spuds left over from the main planting, try a couple in tubs or even in a decent-sized hanging basket. Or what about the drum from an old spin dryer or washing machine? Or a low stack made from two or three old car tyres? Use maincrop seed for this. The technique for tub or stack growing is to plant a spud (or two) into a layer of composty soil, and cover with more soil. Let the leaves grow through. When they're a few inches high, bury them under a couple more inches of soil. Repeat. If you leave them time to get a bit of strength, the leaves will continue to grow up through each new covering layer. When they reach the top, leave them be. With luck, the plants will have set little tubers all up their deep stem. Keep the tub well-watered at all times, and get the soil mix as rich as you can. Harvest when the flowers appear. With a bit of ingenious protection you can keep the plant growing well into the autumn, or even later if the insulation is good.

You can sow spring cabbage in summer, for early greens the following spring. Where will you plant them? First choice is Patch C, for brassicas, but you could also plant some in Patch B, the patch to which brassicas will be moving the following year. Rotations are meant to be a help to disease resistance, not an inexorable law. It's fine to overlap, as long as you keep the principle in mind. And if you do have clubroot problems, play safe.

Believe it or not, there is a variety of kale which you can allegedly grow to make walking-sticks from. I've never tried it, but I can well believe it. A hobby for the kids?

Which leads on to what is known in the veg trade as 'queer gear'. This is a flexible term. When we first came to rural West Wales, garlic was pretty QG, and courgettes certainly were. Endive, rocket, chicory, and radicchio were also unheard of. I guess they are all pretty well-known now. These days QG would probably include celtuce, stripey tomatoes, tomatillos, salsify, scorzonera, and many other odd-ball crops that the private gardener can grow, or at least have a bash at growing for himself. Don't rush in, though. Just try one or two at a time. Salsify, incidentally, is sometimes called 'vegetable oyster', but I have always found it quite pleasant. It's worth growing for its flowers alone.

There are other organic soil additives and plant fertilisers that might come in useful. Seaweed, 'calcified' or straight (although there is some concern that the calcified granules dredged up from the seabed might have been over-harvested); dried blood; bone meal; hoof and horn meal; bracken... Liquid seaweed is very handy, especially as a foliar feed.

Wood chippings make terrific mulch. A mulch is a layer of anything that you lay on the surface, either to keep weeds down (black plastic or old carpets, for example) or as a slow release fertiliser or soil conditioner (leafmould or straw, say). Chippings have the wonderful advantage of being both an excellent weed-suppressant when raw and a soil conditioner when they have rotted down. But don't dig them in when raw, as the rotting process robs the soil of nitrogen. Surface rotting is fine. It will take years though, so be prepared to rake the chippings to one side until needed again if you want to access the soil beneath them. You could also use chippings to keep the paths between your beds weed- and mud-free. Of course, when thoroughly rotted you can compost them, or add direct to the beds. Repeat.

If you like the idea of chippings, try contacting your local electricity board to find out who keeps their lines clear for them. These companies send out vans with teams to hack back invasive shrubs and saplings, which they then feed straight into a massive and noisy shredder. They will probably be happy to deliver half a ton if you ask nicely, or are prepared to pay a little for the delivery. Try the Council, too.

If you have any sort of horsey establishment nearby, do take as much muck as they can offer, and also ask about 'spoiled hay'. Horses need top stuff. If their hay has got stale, or damp, the owners might be keen to get rid of it. Use it as a mulch, or add it in layers into the compost, watering as you go, and making sure plenty of juicy stuff goes in as well. Over winter, the mulch hay will begin to break down but it will probably take another year or two to break down completely, Keep forking it about from job to job. Eventually it will incorporate itself. NB Slugs will enjoy hiding under hay mulch. Is this a problem? Of course not. It's an opportunity... Release the ducks!! Or, failing that, take down your razor on a stick... or whatever. Perhaps you will collect the critters in a paper bag and release them in a local woodland.

Nicotine was once used as a pesticide, but it is a very powerful poison and dangerous stuff. No doubt it is illegal as well. Just so you know.

Maybe you can find local sources of lime (calcium carbonate). Eggshells from a cake bakery, seashells (although it's probably illegal to take them off a beach), old lime mortar off old bricks (but not cement). Is there a limestone quarry nearby? Would they let you fill a bag or two with dust? Or gravelly bits you can hammer to a coarse powder?

It has been claimed that organic broad beans, being more healthily raised, resist leaf-nibbling weevils simply because their leaves are strong and tough, and thus too much like hard work for those nasty little weevily teeth. Whether this is true or not, I couldn't say, but it is an example of what organic growing is about: soil in fine fettle will grow strong plants and strong plants are bound to be more pest resistant than those brought up on burgers and fries.

I think I've mentioned this before, but remember that 'early' just means 'quicker but lighter cropping' when referring to seeds. Use early spuds to beat blight... and early carrots for a late planting, or a late (June) planting to help against carrot root fly. What other variations might you come up with for your own circumstances, particularly if you have some cloches or other protection?

Hardening off...

If you are short of protection, and floor space even, and have plants growing on in small pots, you can knock up a useful hardening unit:

Fix a batten to a house wall facing the sun. Hang half fruit juice boxes along the batten, leaving modest gaps between them. (Cut each box on a gentle diagonal to make two open boxes with high backs: easier for applying clout nails or staples.) Drop a small pot containing a plant you want to harden off into each of these boxes. The boxes will distort quite easily and take bigger pots than you think.

Cover with bubble wrap for the first night or two, or all day if it's suddenly turned cold. How you do this, I leave to you.

The house wall will help to keep the plants a little warmer than the air outside. Don't forget to keep the plants well watered. After 2-3 days of no protection, move them out into the wilds. Keep a closer eye than normal on something that's just been planted out, as it will still be a bit flabby from its cosseted life on the hearthrug, so to speak.

Something we've found very useful is a long measuring stick made from an 8 foot bamboo, with wraps of insulation tape at 6, 12 or 15 inch intervals. This is not because we want to plant our courgettes or onions out with military precision, but because after a few plants you sometimes find your judgement of spacing begins to wander. It's all too easy for 12 inches to have shrunk to 6 inches by the time you get to the end of a row or bed. If you are feeling particularly creative or frivolous you could use different coloured tapes for different spacings on the same bamboo. We once had one with four different colours on it. Very, very attractive, and worth a couple of free pints if you take it down to the pub and leave it casually propped against the bar.

While you're finding your feet, you will no doubt find that odd bare patches turn up on your plots which you hadn't bargained for. For example, what happens after the onions or spuds are lifted? What goes onto that bare patch? Is it possible to grow a 'catch crop', perhaps under some sort of tunnel cloche protection? Of course, you can always green manure it, but if a bit of extra crop is possible, still working within the rotation system, well, why not? Perhaps you've had something growing on in cells or pots for just this occasion?

***

Now for the weirdo stuff...

It is a fact well-known to scientists that every atom and every molecule has its own vibratory rate. The phenomenon of vibration is also well known to mystics and metaphysicians. Dowsers and psychometrists also refer to it.

Once you look beneath the surface of the apparent physical world, vibration makes an appearance. A vibration is a curious and complex event. There must be something to vibrate, a pole about which the vibration takes place, and a controlling agent or power of some kind to control the rate of vibration, and which presumably sets it off in the first place. Science has no idea what this power might be. Thus, vibration is a mystery, and thus all the paranormal experimenters above cannot just be written off as superstitious fools when they speak of 'personal vibrations'. Perhaps they actually know something the scientists don't. It wouldn't be the first time.

Psychics of all kinds maintain that each person and living thing has its own personal vibe. Some vibes are harmonious with another individual's and some are not. This is why some people are immediately attracted to each other, and others are not, they say. The psychedelic culture of the 1960s was very keen on exploring these ideas. Remember *Good Vibrations*?

So... given that vibrations are unexplained by science, the weirdo stuff below might yet turn out to be eminently sensible. Time will tell.

There are two immediate aspects of 'weird' gardening behaviour that occasionally fill the 'and finally' slot on the news: talking to plants and playing them music. I cringe when I see the cosy, knowing expressions on the faces of tv presenters when they talk about Prince Charles, the well-known loony, talking to his plants. But experiments have been done, most recently by the Royal Horticultural Society, no less, which suggest that plants *do* respond to being talked to. Other experiments have shown that plants *do* grow better when played music... and that they prefer Mozart or Ravi Shankar to raucous rock music. In fact 'acid rock' stunts them. (One wonders what it does to the musicians.)

What's going on here? Do plants really understand human speech? Or the intricacies of a raga? Or are they somehow picking up and harmonising with some sort of emotional vibration? It's my guess that it's the latter. This 'sympathetic vibration' would begin to explain that other well-known phenomenon of 'green fingers'. The people who grew huge cabbages virtually on the beaches of Findhorn in northern Scotland had interesting views on all this. More details in Chapter 19.

The Findhorn experience is based upon person-to-plant communication. The proof of the effect lies in the huge crops they achieved. Many a gardener and farmer also knows that there is something in this. What we need is for a totally unbiased research institute to carry out a full programme of carefully controlled experiments. But this is unlikely to happen any time soon, because guess who funds most of the research institutes? Yes, it's *CrappoChemInc*, and they are certainly not going to pay for research that just might put them out of a job and release their hard-earned stranglehold on people's food supply. But one day... and maybe you are the man or woman, dear reader, who will set the ball rolling.

Meanwhile, there is a mode of farming and gardening called 'biodynamics' which I found quite laughable when I first came across it, as it deals with things like phases of the moon, and extraordinary potions involving (among other things) cow horn, quartz dust, and stag bladders.

However, there is a large number of professional farmers, particularly on the continent, including several hard-nosed Burgundian wine-growers, who are making a fine living following the doctrine of biodynamics. Whether you like it or not, it works. *Why* it works is another matter, of course. I never had the time to experiment with biodynamics, but a friend of mine did. He is a hard-headed farmer, who grows carrots expertly, and by the field-full. One year he planted half his crop as normal, and the other half according to the biodynamic moon schedule. To his surprise the biodynamic ones cropped considerably better.

If you are feeling experimental, *The Secret Life of Plants* and *Secrets of the Soil* will give you plenty of ideas (see Chapter 19).

***

Back to strict practicality.... *Get a tetanus jab*. Soil is a whole universe of tiny entities, each with its own life plan. I don't suppose they mean you any personal harm, but some of these entities can be dangerous if they get under your skin. If you have a cut on your hand, make sure it is well protected before getting down to the soil. Wear gloves when possible, I would say. And be safe in the knowledge that should you accidentally fall bum-first onto your rake (somebody somewhere will have done it) your anti-tetanus jab will protect you, at least from lock-jaw, if not from embarrassment and draughty whotsits, and the hysterical shrieks and finger-pointing of any witnesses, spouses, children, nurses, surgeons etc who become involved.

It's also not a bad idea to invest in a pair of really heavy-duty thick leather gloves, as well as the usual nancy little 'gardening gloves'. Once in a while, you will be glad you bought them, even if only for escorting chopped off tendrils of brambles to the bonfire. Once the fire is good, hot green brambles burn well, incidentally.

Chapter 18
Cooperation and Sharing

This going to be another short chapter, as most of what it contains can be reduced to a few words: 'We're all in this together, so share the bounty, and be the happier for it'.

First of all, we organic types aim to work as closely with Nature as we can, rather than battering her about with poisons and chemicals. We use 'appropriate technology', which means the smallest tool or machine that will do the job rather than over-powered monsters of any type. If possible, we work by hand, to maintain the peace of the garden and to fully enjoy the miracles around us.

Working on the principle of 'lowest technology possible' I discovered to my own surprise that I could weed between our long beds more quickly with a 'push hoe' than with the rotavator. A push hoe is an arrow-shaped blade attached to a jig with a wheel in the front and push-along handles at the back. No engine; just accurately applied push-force, using the ancient principle of leverage. A good model is incredibly efficient and will even lift turf if you are feeling strong and there's no football on the telly.

The push hoe is silent, wastes no fossil fuels, and won't suddenly lurch into the crop if it hits a big stone. It will also nip in and out close to large plants to trim off weeds that the rotavator could never reach. Neither does it ever break down, and it can be left out in the rain all week if necessary. A wonderful tool for a large veg plot. It also keeps you fit. What more do you want?

My point being that we should experiment extensively with lo-tec tools before rushing out to buy gimmicky or unnecessarily hi-tec ones. Lo-tec is always greener, and thus more in harmony with Nature.

Organic types also cooperate with the soil, boosting its powers at every opportunity. In return, the soil gives us

stronger and more pest-resistant crops which are also more flavoursome and nutritious than the poor pale stuff from *Crappo*.

We cooperate with helpful insects by not using powerful biocides which kill indiscriminately. We also encourage beneficial insects by planting flowers and leaving the odd nettle and weed in situ. Even surface stones can supply shelter to helpful beetles (...and slugs. Traps for free!)

We discourage attack in advance, rather than react to it, by leaving the soil surface dry if possible, so that slugs can't get to our plants. We put barriers round the carrots, and round cabbage roots. And we are constantly looking for tweaks and bright ideas which will cut down on work and cost while doing the job better. Plastic milk cartons and jam jars as mini-cloches; milk cartons, trimmed suitably, as plant pots; trimmed and nailed to a batten on a wall as a flower and herb trough; de-capped and half-buried, as watering aids; de-capped and carefully angled, baited, and propped, as a mouse trap (yes, it works...); etc, etc...

We naturally extend this spirit of cooperation into the animal world. We put up bird tables, hang out fat, erect bird baths and so on. The cooperative element means that if you look after the birds, the birds will repay you by eating a lot of bugs which might otherwise help you out with your cabbages. Nest boxes will encourage local populations to stay local.

Clearly, there are limits to this process. If it were possible to cooperate with rabbits, I would be delighted to do so. 'These are for you, Flopsy; those are for me. Deal?' But it doesn't seem to work that way. However, I bet somebody somewhere has worked something out. The Findhorn experience may be a pointer (see Chapter 19).

The key word in all this is 'balance'. It would be disastrous if we were to kill off *all* the aphids, as small birds would then starve. Nature is in a constant flux of shifting and self-regulating balances. We are a part of this system. If we upset it too much, we will be sure to pay the price. Cause leads to effect.

In China, in the 1960s, Chairman Mao became concerned

that sparrows were eating a lot of the nation's grain crop before it could be harvested. His solution was to mobilise the whole population. Millions of people spent several days chivvying sparrows from dawn till dusk, allowing them no rest. Eventually, they fell exhausted from the sky in their tens of millions. The problem was solved. The following year, the grain fields were infested with bugs and weevils.

The prime causes of unrest in the world are greed, tribalism, and separatism. These are three faces of the one problem: selfishness, born of fear. The more we can accept that we are essentially one family and can share the world's bounty, the more peace will become the norm and not the exception, and governments can stop squandering half our tax money on weapons. We can each do our bit to develop a cooperative and sharing attitude, especially veg growers, and organic veg growers in particular.

Why not make a point of giving away, say 5% of your crop? Share with a neighbour; especially with someone elderly or incapacitated. A local priest of whatever denomination will be able to put you in touch with someone who would be grateful. If you are C of E and the needy party is a Muslim or a Rasta, so much the better. If you are agnostic or a humanist or a vehement atheist, it is all the same.

Can you set up a modest box scheme to sell any surplus crop? You don't need to become a greengrocer. Just offer what you have, when you have it, and at a reasonable price, or for free if you fancy it. People will be glad to have any fresh, local food, especially if you can certify it as organic (see Chapter 19). Perhaps as you go you might find people who want to grow a bit of their own but who have no garden, and also people who have a garden who would like to have someone grow a few veg in it. Just go out and 'connect'.

If you can't do a box scheme on your own, perhaps you could pal up with a couple of other allotmenteers or similar.

Or you could put a local box scheme grower or farmer in touch with people who would like him to visit them.

Simplest of all for many people is to just shop as much as

possible at a farmers' market. These are usually weekly affairs, run by farmers selling direct to the public, thus cutting out the leeching middlemen. You won't find every single thing you 'need' there, but you will find a lot of good stuff, and maybe you'll discover you don't actually need much of that other stuff you thought you needed. Pick organic wherever possible, but even if there isn't much organic available, at least you'll be paying the farmer a proper price rather than the pittance he would get from *Crappo*. See if you can work out some bulk discounts and buy for a couple of friends at the same time. And you could always tell the farmer you'd be very interested in buying more off him if he were organically certified.

Could you drop off a couple of kilos of carrots or a cabbage or two at your local school or hospital or hospice? Just for the joy of it?

You could help get some decent food to other people by buying spuds six sacks at a time from your local organic grower or farmer. He'll probably offer you a discount. Accept it joyfully, and give him a fancy squash in return. Give him the squash anyway, discount or not. Keep one sack and sell the other five to neighbours to pay for your petrol. Everyone's a winner.

Share your knowledge, especially in the veg growing area. Encourage other people to grow their own as well. Take a little time to demonstrate. Invite people round to see how you do it.

And why stop there? Consumerism and endless advertising has fragmented what were once healthily inter-acting societies into isolated consumer units, either at work, which they are usually less than enthusiastic about, or glued to their trash-filled screens at home.

Can you offer to share your other skills, for free, with someone? A postcard in the Post Office window, or its equivalent, offering a couple of free basic lessons in how to use the internet or a digital camera, particularly for pensioners or other people who feel they've been left behind in the digital revolution?

Could you teach a couple of teenagers how to knit? (Or ask for someone to teach *you*?)

Or how to make delicious bread in the microwave? (See Chapter 19)

Or teach a bit of conversational English to an immigrant?

We can all help each other in some way, and we really need to get back into the habit, and heal our society. If we don't, we are doomed to ever-increasing feelings of loneliness and pointlessness, which will inevitably lead to more fear and anger and well... you know the rest. Violence, drug addiction... and paranoia all round.

It needn't be like that. Go on... make a difference! Start the ball rolling! Soon, others will join in. The internet may be a useful ally if you want to reach young people and get them engaged. Many young people need to get engaged, and to find some creative point to their impoverished, consumerised lives. Many of them would love to grow a few plants, even if they don't yet know it.

Some people who are already doing this sort of thing are the guerrilla gardeners. Visit them at www.guerrillagardening.org – wonderful stuff... and www.incredible-edible-todmorden. co.uk too.

No doubt these, and other pioneering groups, would be happy to help you to develop an initiative of your own.

You might also like to consider a sort of 'remote sharing' with the rest of humanity by reconsidering how much meat you eat. In a 2006 report, the United Nations disclosed that livestock is responsible for 18% of greenhouse gas emissions... more than *all* transport put together (13%). What's more, the methane that is burped and farted into the atmosphere is over 20 times more damaging than CO_2, the usual culprit, and it is getting worse by the year. Most of the destruction of the Amazon rain forest is to graze cattle for beefburgers (for a year or two before the soil washes away). At the moment we in the UK eat twice as much meat as we used to in the 1960s, and the rate of consumption is increasing.

Paul McCartney is suggesting we could each start to tackle this absurd situation by having a 'Meat-free Monday'. If you find you don't immediately drop dead because of this lack

of meat, you might consider a 'Meat-free Thursday' as well...
What do you think?

Just as a matter of interest, we found that our own home-grown veg was so delicious that we spontaneously cut down on meat anyway, and went for considerable periods as vegetarians. And we didn't drop dead, I can now report.

Chapter 19
Help and Support

The first thing a new organic gardener should do is to consider joining *Garden Organic*. This splendid organisation is, I believe, the biggest organic research association in Europe, if not the world. It was originally set up in the 1950s by Lawrence D Hills (see his book below) who called it the *Henry Doubleday Research Association* (or *HDRA*). It has since attracted 40,000+ members and is growing apace as more and more people seriously question what *CrappoUnlimited* is serving us as food.

Visit www.gardenorganic.org.uk

Or ring 0247 630 3517

GO publishes an informative quarterly magazine, and a useful website, and has a problem-solving service for members. They also have a beautiful organic garden cum educational site at Ryton-on-Dunsmore, near Coventry. Well worth a visit, if only for the superb food in the café and restaurant.

The other organisation you should know about and might like to consider joining is the *Soil Association*. In a world of chancers and slippery businessmen, the *SA* has done a sterling job in getting the word 'organic' legally protected. Thus, anything you see with the word 'organic' attached to it *must* have been raised in accordance with agreed 'organic' standards. If you call something 'organic' which does not meet these standards, you are breaking the law. It's worth pointing this out to those purveyors of sad plants at boot sales, labelled 'organic', when what they mean is 'mainly neglected but with just a bit of chemical fertiliser to help it along'.

If you want a legal 'organic' licence you must be personally inspected by the *SA*, which costs somewhere around £500 a year, a fortune for small growers or allotmenteers. In my view this inspection is pretty much unnecessary, not least because it puts a lot of people off joining up. I would prefer to see a mentoring system whereby a new candidate is passed over to an existing member, who susses the new bloke out. The mentor would tell very quickly whether the newcomer was a genuine person or a rip-off merchant looking to cheat his way into a few quick 'organic' bucks. Inspections can't check character nearly as well as a sustained period of mentoring can. Mentoring would be much cheaper, too, and would put the 'certified organic' label within the reach of every gardener who wanted it.

If you can't face the expense of paying for an official *SA* inspection, and still want to sell some of your crop as 'organic', bill it as 'Grown in accordance with *SA* organic standards'. You might add 'Please come and visit us, to check how we grow your food.' Get people *involved*... Maybe even invite them to help with the work, learning as they go.

The above assumes that you know what the *SA* standards are, and that you have indeed stuck to them. Roughly speaking, if you stick to the principles included in this book, you will be up to *SA* standards. If you want to read their full standards, ring and ask, or visit www.soilassociation.org/organicstandards
...or phone: 0117 314 5000
I'm pretty sure that if you've gone to the trouble of buying and reading this book that you will stick to the standards on principle. Over to you.

Join a local gardening club. Clubs are always great places

for support. If there isn't one, start one. It's easy. Print a few flyers and distribute them frugally and wisely, especially to a few popular and suitable shop windows, and send a copy, along with a nice letter, to the local paper. If you can provide a 'photo opportunity' so much the better. Any sort of gimmick that photographs well will do. A basket of red chard, yellow tomatoes and purple peppers will do the trick every time, accompanied by a placard stating 'Grow Your Own!', and a winning smile. Everybody looks at photos, especially if they show someone smiling and holding something. I'm sure you can think of other suitable photo ops.

Your local radio station will be interested, too. Prepare a little 30-second speech on how lots of people want to grow a bit of veg but don't know how. 'We want to change that...' and see what develops via the presenter's questions. Try to pre-empt as many questions as possible and have your responses ready. Make sure the listeners know exactly how to contact you too.

Any club, old or new, is a wonderful source of help, advice, free plants and seeds and seedlings (but beware of tainted brassicas), and the occasional shoulder to cry on. Old clubs will have a lot of Blast Everything With Chemicals supporters. They are the dinosaurs. Be kind to them and give them an organic lettuce. They may even change their mind one day, and you will have helped in that process. Good for you.

There are of course, numerous websites and gardening-related chat rooms out there in cyberspace. Take your pick, and don't take anyone's word as Gospel.

One interesting site belongs to the *National Society of Allotment and Leisure Gardeners*, who claim that 'Every council is duty bound to provide 20 allotments per 1,000 residents. It is up to people to put pressure on the authorities to move things along.' This means nagging councillors and MPs, writing to the press, ringing up the local radio people and hanging round in town centres with banners and leaflets, and a petition for people to sign, asking for an allotment of their own. It will also help if you can come up with a few places where you think new allotments might usefully be founded. Invite your councillors to meet you on site at the best place, and invite the press along as well. If the councillors don't turn up, the press have got a story. If they do turn up, they will be obliged to say something positive, and will know they have gone on record. Keep the pressure up. Keep plugging the words 'organic' and 'sustainable'. The press will be on your side. Keep them well informed, regularly.

Visit other gardens and allotments. Look carefully, and ask questions. Don't believe the answers, but keep an open mind. Why are his beetroot healthier looking than yours? Why are your onions bigger than hers? Look at spacings, ask more questions. What varieties? Any views on other varieties? What's his soil like? What does he add to it?

Varieties are regional and as every garden is different in its soil values, you may find your peas are far better than your neighbour's, but his courgettes thrive while yours refuse to.

Most gardeners are chemically inclined. Their crops will often look fine and may exceed yours in size. They may even taste as good in certain cases. But appearances can be deceptive. All that glisters is not gold. Naturally grown food will be richer in vitamins and trace elements than chemically grown food.

In the case of vitamins, good food contains all you need. *CrappoGalactico* know this, and it delights them that they can make enormous profits from selling you depleted foods because *then* they can make even more profits by selling you quite unnecessary vitamin pills to make up for the depleted food. This is what the bean-counters call a win-win situation. It's what any sane intelligence calls a 'lose-lose' one. One can only hope that a visiting Martian would shake her heads in disbelief, and move on elsewhere.

The UK spends £330,000,000 every year on vitamins, almost all of it wasted. If we had proper food...

Read a few books, but don't get over-excited or frightened by the authors' enthusiasms or dire warnings. The only absolute rule in gardening is: help the seed to grow. Spacing, timing, watering, feeding... a book can give a rough guide, possibly, but not The Truth. You must learn The Truth for your own plot as you get to know it and work with it.

Here are a few books I would recommend to anyone:

Lawrence D Hills: *Grow Your Own Fruit and Vegetables*
John Seymour: *The Complete Food Garden*
Piers Warren: *How to Store Your Garden Produce*
Bob Flowerdew: *Bob Flowerdew's Organic Bible: Successful Gardening the Natural Way*

And, as previously mentioned...

Pauline Pears and Bob Sherman: *Pests – How to Control them on Fruit and Vegetables*
George Pilkington: *Composting with Worms*
Mike Woolnough: *Worms and Wormeries*
Graham Harvey: *We Want Real Food*

If you are prepared to be scared witless by all the horrors that might befall your little plants, Dr DG Hessayon's *Be Your Own Vegetable Doctor* is worth a look. The illustrations and descriptions of a thousand ghastly ills are very helpful, but his treatments tend very strongly towards the Nuke The Lot school of thought.

There are many others. And don't forget that any gardening book at all, particularly Edwardian or Victorian ones, will contain odd gems that might be of use to you. Read; consider; adapt...

And get a book on wild flowers (the more respectful name for weeds) and another on garden insects. And perhaps one on birds. There seem to be lots to choose from these days. The Readers' Digest *Wildflowers of Britain* is very good, as is the Octopus *Wild Flowers*; if you can find them. There is a comprehensive, astonishing, and occasionally terrifying, insect book called *Insects*, published by Hamlyn.

***

If you'd like to see how one family set up and ran a modest organic smallholding from scratch, you could try my own *Scenes from a Smallholding* and *More Scenes from a*

Smallholding. If you approve of Fairtrade, you might like to buy copies direct from the author at www.thirdleafbooks.co.uk (*More Scenes...* even tells how to make bread in a microwave. It's dead easy, and great bread.)

Any organic or 'greenie' person should investigate permaculture...
http://www.permaculture.org.uk/mm.asp?mmfile=whatispermaculture
http://www.growveg.com/growguides/permaculture.aspx

...and also a school of gardening dedicated to 'no dig' principles, which is an extension of growing in beds and using mulches as weed suppressants, so you don't need to dig and disturb the soil structure at all.
Try http://www.primalseeds.org/OTHERSTUFF/new/nodig.htm

***

Another vital connection must be with *Chase Organics,* the people who produce the most comprehensive and helpful seed catalogue in the business, in association with *Garden Organic.* You name it, they stock it, and suggest ways of growing it. They also advise between varieties, and offer lots of helpful tips.
www.OrganicCatalogue.com
...or ring 0845 130 1304
They also sell books, tools, organic fertilisers, flower seeds (including bee, butterfly and bat mixtures), mushroom kits, propagators, cold frames, cloches and small polytunnels; *and* an intriguing selection of 'biological controls': tiny parasites and predators which will help to keep your pest levels down without chemicals. One will even kill caterpillars on cabbages, although it's not as satisfying as picking them off with tweezers and passing them over to a duck. Not that the duck is likely to eat them, but at least they'll drop them on the floor away from the cabbage leaf.

***

If, like me, you find the whole extraordinary process of plant growth vanishingly unlikely, you might like to read a couple of books which try to look beneath the surface.

Top of the list comes *The Findhorn Garden*, written by 'the Findhorn community'. It tells the tale of how a small group of people set up a garden on the sandy gravel of a northern Scottish coastline. When they arrived, only coarse grasses could scrape a living. Yet these people succeeded in growing a bounteous garden which baffled the experts, who could not explain how 4olb cabbages and 8 foot high delphiniums could possibly grow there. It is a remarkably thought-provoking book, involving as it does, concepts that are very alien to many of us.

There is another book on Findhorn, written by a sceptical visitor, Paul Hawken: *The Magic of Findhorn*. This is worth a read, too. He came away a changed man.

If the Findhorn experience whets your appetite for deeper causes and meaning, you will thoroughly enjoy *The Secret Life of Plants*, and *Secrets of the Soil*, both by Peter Tompkins and Christopher Bird.

I can't recommend these two books highly enough if you have an enquiring mind.

You might like to add *Why Us?* by Dr James LeFanu, which points out that the mechanistic Scientific Materialist philosophy which underpins all our medical and farming practices should be seriously questioned, as recent research shows it to be deeply flawed.

Chapter 20
A Few Final Thoughts

The key to organic growing, and indeed an 'organic lifestyle', to use a word I normally hate, is to work with, and not against, Nature.

When we work peacefully with Nature we create beautiful parks and gardens. When we attack instead, we create deserts and dustbowls. As examples, Kansas in the 1930s; and the Amazon and Indonesian rainforests today; and large areas of our oceans as well: just google the North Pacific Gyre, to get a glimpse of the vast scale of the problem.

When we first moved to the country, we wanted to be as organic and as self-sufficient as possible, but I was always quite sure that if our crops were threatened with total devastation and that we would thus have no food (we had no back-up money to buy our groceries from *CrappoGigaMarts* instead...), and if I was convinced that chemical pest-killers would save the day, then I would use the chemicals. I don't see the point in being a politically correct corpse.

However... over the fifteen years we spent running our organic smallholding, growing commercial vegetable crops to boot, I never once needed the chemicals. Well, once, actually. We had a colony of slugs that were devastating some of our household seedlings in a polytunnel. We locked the tunnel down, so that no wildlife could get in, and scattered a few pellets round the most vulnerable plants. Next morning I removed 43 corpses and we had no further trouble, except from mice who would dig up the courgette seeds, eat the kernels, and leave the husks in tidy piles for us next morning. The only way we could think of to deal with this one was trapping. And I shot one.

We had crop failures, of course, some trivial and some absolute, but somehow we always got by and increased our harvest in proportion to our developing skills. We proved to

ourselves that food *can* be grown organically, and on a useful scale. We've also met a number of highly skilled organic growers and farmers who make a proper living growing organically.

The future for feeding the world lies not in genetic tinkering, which will bring short-term benefits only to the techno-business multinationals, suicide to many thousands more indigenous peasant farmers, and leave us with unpredictable and polluted genomes in our food crops. Instead, the future lies in a global return to respect: respect for the soil, Nature, living things, and each other. There is already plenty of food in the world to feed everyone adequately. Everyone agrees on this. What is needed is the social and political will to share the world's freely-given bounty a little more fairly. Who needs bloated billionaires? Who needs starving millions? There must be a better way...

And there is. All it requires is for each one of us who understands the nature of the problem to do a little personal something about it. Growing our own quality food is an excellent first step... showing someone else how to do the same is the second.

Every new movement begins small. Be overjoyed to be a part of it, and bear in mind that the government expects quite a few hectares of 'prairie' farmland in East Anglia to not be growing stuff in the foreseeable future, because of gluts in grain production. That means there is plenty of land potentially available for small growers using less-land-intensive organic methods, if only they had access to it.

Well, maybe there *is* a way for them to gain access, by buying a few hectares at a time from the present owners. Perhaps as a cooperative? And maybe we could repopulate East Anglia en route! Has anyone ever considered this possibility? (If this idea interests you, take a look at *More Scenes from a Smallholding*.) How many unused hectares are we talking about here, do you think? A thousand? Ten thousand?

How about *two hundred thousand*? That's *half a million* acres that could be growing healthy veg but which is instead doing nothing, as of 2010. 'Go figure', as I'm sure someone must have said.

Meanwhile, on your own modest plot: observe, note, learn,

be patient... and don't take any expert's word as absolute truth...

Above all... enjoy it! Even when a rabbit has bitten off every single cabbage plant overnight... think 'What have we got here? A tragedy? No! It's a *learning opportunity!*' and then feel really, really smug because you know you've got a reserve batch of seedlings coming on in the shed. *And* you found some particularly fragrant dog poo in the park yesterday which you can smear here and there where you think the rabbit is getting in. But do wear gloves, won't you? Heavens...

I wish you endless joy in your gardening. Spend as little as possible on it. Be creative! Be beautiful! Be happy! And enjoy the strawberries!

Chas Griffin
Newcastle Emlyn
West Wales 2011

Postscript

I've just been clearing out some old files and came across a useful letter to the editor of possibly the *Daily Telegraph*. It must be at least twenty years old.

In it, the writer laments the destruction of so many fertile allotments: prime growing land built over for 'cheap' housing and leisure centres and so forth, and reminds us of how productive an allotment can be.

In good hands, he says, a standard allotment of one sixteenth of an acre (as a gauge, a football pitch needs about two acres and a golf course 200-300 acres) will produce, if well cared for and properly fertilised with compost:

Carrots	28lb
Parsnips	75lb
Beet	86lb
Lettuce	280 heads
Radish	24 bunches
Broad beans	24lb
Peas	45lb
Cabbage	66 heads
Cabbage (spring)	108 heads
Brussel sprouts	35lb
Turnips	29lb
Runner beans	61lb
Dwarf beans	19lb
Cabbage (Savoy)	66 heads
Marrows	24
Onions	192lb
Spring onions	20 bunches
Parsley	as required
Potatoes (early)	84lb
Potatoes (maincrop)	410lb
Leeks	96
Broccoli	130 heads
Celery	48 heads
Swedes	44lb

Tomatoes	120lb
Gooseberries	18lb
Rhubarb	7lb
Cucumbers	20

There are roughly two lbs to a kilo.

This is a colossal amount of food. Just look at it carefully for a moment and consider how much your household uses in a week. Would ~250 kg of spuds last an entire year? It might, or at least for as long as they remain wholesome in store. A whole lettuce every day of the season with plenty to spare for friends! At current prices, something like £100 worth of broccoli. More cabbage than you can shake a rake at!

Are the numbers accurate? I can't swear to it, but the letter-writer was clearly someone who had gone to the trouble of noting down his crop weights, so I suspect he was meticulous in his gardening as well. I certainly wouldn't call the list and the quantities fairy tales. I *know* that a small plot, carefully tended, will produce crops at a far higher rate than a farm does. You will come to know this too. All it needs is enthusiasm, common sense and quite a bit of thoughtfully-applied honest to goodness effort, and I wouldn't be a bit surprised if your own allotment or garden was producing top rate food in similar quantities within a year or two.

You've already done the hardest bit, reading this book.

Well what are you waiting for? Get planning...

Post postscript

A Few Rather Jumbled Tips for Would-be Smallholders

First of all... having a crack at smallholding is more than just an interesting challenge and opportunity for personal growth; it is also a small but vital contribution towards the world's increasingly disrupted and damaged ecology.

Every *month* millions of tons of topsoil are lost to the world through bad farming practices, largely in the 'developed' world. As the humus is robbed out, by the application of ever greater tonnages of fertilisers, the soils lose their friability and structure, and revert to powdered rock. This stuff can no longer retain water or microlife, and it either washes away or blows away. And once it's lost.. it stays lost.

The greatest crisis facing mankind is going to be the wastage of proper land to grow his food on, never mind the greenhouse effects etc brought on by wastage of fuel resources.

You good people will be doing your bit: treating your little parish of soil with respect, and putting back into it as much as you possibly can. If everyone did what you are about to do, there would never be a soil crisis, would there?

It never ceases to amaze and alarm me how few people connect consumerism with pollution and eco-destruction. I'm sure you already have this one properly sussed, but just in case:

Every item you buy, from a potato to a dishwasher, has needed various blasts of energy in order to get it into your kitchen. Some of these blasts are very large, and *every* blast of energy used has released greenhouse gases into the atmosphere. Electricity itself is made from coal or gas, which when burned chuck out clouds of polluting gases. (Nuclear electricity is different, of course, producing no direct greenhouse gases, but instead extremely dangerous residues that will remain so for millennia.)

The potato you bought from *CrappoMegaBux* has required energy to move it as 'seed' from its home (probably in Scotland) to the farmer's land. The 'seed' was then planted by a machine towed by a tractor. The tractor and machine both required huge amounts of energy to make them, and the tractor uses diesel and oils to keep it going. The spuds are then junkied along with artificial fertilisers (which need energy to derive them from the oil products they are made from) and blasted with various biocides (all requiring lots of energy to make and package and deliver). Each spraying uses more tractor diesel and oil.

The spuds are then mechanically lifted (more oil energy), sorted (on a mechanical conveyor which needs energy to make and operate it), washed with expensively purified water in another energy-expensive machine and bagged (more energy to make, print, and deliver the bags, particularly if they are made of oil-derived plastics). The bags are then strapped onto pallets (more energy to make and deliver the pallets, nails, strapping, etc) and trucked off to the supermarkets (more diesel).

The final energy blast comes from your good selves when you drive to the shop and home again.

All this for a humble potato which does at least serve a vital purpose in feeding someone.

Now consider a dishwasher!

Just about every energy input for the potato will be required, but this time on a massive scale. Then there are other energy costs to add: the metals, plastics, rubbers, greases, paints and papers must all be made in factories which use huge quantities of energy and pump out huge quantities of bad stuff into the air and rivers. All these raw materials must be shifted (more pallets, boxes, diesel) to other factories for forming into components for the machine (more huge quantities of energy and pollution), then shifted again (boxes, pallets, diesel...) to the company factory where they are assembled, using... yes, lots more energy.

Then the finished machines are packed into boxes (all that oil-derived polystyrene), the instruction booklets are added (which took more energy to produce the paper and ink, then the moving of the paper and ink, then the printing, and the moving of the finished booklets...) and they are strapped onto pallets and loaded into trucks, whence they are shifted yet again, to your local store. You add the final blast by driving to the store to examine the product, and possibly driving it home yourself. And once you switch it on, you use yet more electricity (which means yet more pollution) and gallons of expensive water.

And all this... using thousands of times more energy than its equivalent weight of potatoes, for a product that is utterly pointless for most people. Washing up should not be a chore left to one poor sod on his own (her own?), or a daft machine, but a shared experience; the final part of the meal, carefully honed by attention and experience to use the least amount of heat, water and soap to do a thorough job. An enjoyable and creative challenge for all.

We can all save a lot of money and carbon energy by simply thinking through our everyday situation and making adjustments. This attitude will serve you very well on a smallholding, where your potatoes, at least, will require zero input of diesel, once you are growing from your own 'seed'... or seed proper if you get really inspired, and try cross-breeding.

***

Things to talk about well in advance of making the move...

Talk over with your partner and/or family all the aspects of this new life. Why do you want to do it?

To get away from something?
To become as self-sufficient as possible?
To get back in touch with Nature?
To not need to pretend all the time?
To do meaningful work?
To learn new skills?
To become inventive?

To live quietly?
To grow your own food?
To keep animals?
To feed the neighbourhood?

These are all but one very good reasons. Which would you say is the odd one out?

Yes... the top one. If you're trying merely to escape, you will almost certainly find that you will not succeed, as the problem you have lies largely within: 'how you cope with problems'. On a smallholding, you will still have problems, and they may even be more serious or important than the ones you are currently having trouble with. So, if you are trying to escape, think long and hard about the nature of your attitude to problems. If necessary, tackle that issue first.

Personally, I would see the second on the list as being the most positive, but you may not agree, and that's fine.

The notes below are aimed particularly at someone aiming at moderate to serious self-sufficiency, but they apply pretty much as well to anyone else.

***

First: what does 'self-sufficiency' actually mean, to you?

Where do you draw the line (if at all)? Meat? Power? Clothing! Be absolutely honest with yourself and think as clearly as possible. Make notes, and decide where and why you will be drawing that line. In our own case, for example, my wife and I simply wanted to grow organic food for our family, and to grow a cash crop to pay for petrol and so on. Everything else was left fluid.

Next: start getting used to never doing anything on auto.

Begin by challenging your habitual actions, as in: Are my

social habits actually bad habits? Rituals rather than a delight? Am I spending more on *x y* or *z* and enjoying it less? How much of my 'enjoyment' is actually 'routine'? Should I shop elsewhere? If so, why? Are my gadgets or accessories just distractions to stop me feeling utter despair for a little while longer? Why do I buy *this* brand of cosmetic? Really... why? Or *this* brand of electronic gizmo? Am I being suckered here? Am I prepared to go along with this? If so, why?

You get the drift.

You might add some other stuff...

Why do I have or use my current mode of transport? How should I *cost-effectively* recycle more stuff? Why should I make my own jam (or not)? Why should I dynamite the dish-washer (see above for clues) or the telly? Why... should I buy Fairtrade whenever possible, even though it's more expensive? How can I reduce waste in my life? Right down to the smallest detail? (A possibly useful website: http://www.uk.freecycle.org/groups/)

And perhaps...

Why... am I determined to go against the tide of 21ˢᵗ century society in such a head-on manner?

Query *everything* you do, and your motives, and discuss your insights with your family and friends; and never be afraid of any answers you come up with. Questioning your assumptions and prejudices can only be good. (We're just talking 'querying' here: not 'blame' or guilt', which have no place in creative thinking. Honesty is all you need. Some 'prejudices' will turn out to not be prejudices at all, but reasonable judgements based upon past experience. Just be sure to keep things in proportion, and keep smiling. This is meant to be creative and positive!)

If you do discover something startling... well ask yourself 'Why do I find this answer startling?' and calmly think it through. You'll never need a psychiatrist if you can trust yourself to trust yourself. Wisdom begins with self-knowledge, and not much else matters apart from wisdom, the bringer of peace and joy.

If you can't come up with a meaningful answer quickly, just

give it time. Eventually an answer will arrive.

And if the eventual 'answer' is 'Oh!!!... I actually don't *want* to be smallholder, after all. I really want to set up a little bicycle business; or cross the Gobi desert on a walrus; or shed all my pointless responsibilities *somehow*.'

And don't be too surprised if you find en route that a long-held and treasured 'philosophical principle' suddenly appears to be less than the certainty you once thought it to be. Don't defend *any* philosophy (or religion, if it comes to that); *examine* it. If it proves to be valid, great. If not, dump it gratefully and keep seeking.. As Saint Paul, the Buddha, and the Royal Society all say: 'Test everything'.

Money

If you are to have a chance of survival on a very low income (which is what you'll almost certainly be letting yourself in for on a smallholding, as opposed to 'a cottage in the country') then money and debt are terrifically important.

Zero debt is your ideal. If you really can't shake off your mortgage, then make clearing it a top priority. Go without what must be gone without... just get rid of it. If you don't, the usurers will always have you in their power, leeching on your meagre income, and they have no mercy.

Be very sure what money means to you. Is it connected to your sense of self-worth? If so, self-sufficiency of any sort may not yet be for you. Are you lost without your credit card? Ditto. Can you only have fun by spending money? Ditto. Are you lost without 'Labels'? Ditto. Does your car 'say something about you'? Ditto.

Keep a 'penny diary' for a fortnight. Keep track of every single expenditure. Every tiny one. You will soon see where savings can reasonably be made.

Make it a point of honour to save something every week, no matter how cash-strapped you might be. This act of saving is very good for your psychology, as it proves to you that you are not actually as poor as you think... how could you be if you are able to save? It is also good for developing the power of your will... without which nothing positive ever happens.

The savings should be towards specific things, like well-defined treats (see below) or Christmas presents, or whatever you choose. It is remarkable how much a regular contribution can add up to. Just 10p a day equals £36.50 over a year. Quite a sum. Well... it is in my book, anyway!

You can make an excellent money-box from an old biscuit tin, with the lid well and truly gaffer-taped on, coated if necessary with molasses or engine grease, to help reinforce your determination. Obviously you need to whack a small slot in the top. Use an old screwdriver and a hammer, unless your fingernails are particularly well developed.

Where will your 'bill money' come from, once out in the sticks? A cash crop? Or selling skills? Will your skills be marketable? You must be very clear about this from the start and keep a constant eye on the situation, with a back-up clearly in mind. If one scheme fails, you must immediately start on another one. You can *not* afford debt.

If you decide on one or more cash crops (and more than one is definitely a good idea in case one fails badly) then you will need to research your marketing strategy. You will need an extensive and rolling plan.

Ask around in advance and do some calculations (and don't be over-optimistic!). Consider the possibilities of growing decorative plants, flowers or herbs. Again, marketing will be your prime concern: is there a local co-op you could join? What about the internet? We thought garlic would be an excellent cash crop for us for about six reasons (can you think what they were?). However, one particularly awful summer wiped out all 60,000 of our growing stock, so we had to re-think.

Options for generating some cash from normal crops include a Veg Box Scheme round the neighbourhood; selling to neighbours ad hoc; selling to shops; selling at a market stall of your own; adding value yourself, eg by drying or plaiting onions & garlic... but beware: almost any other form of processing (like making chutney or pre-packs) will require all manner of licenses, inspections, and expense. The Veg Box Scheme might be your best bet, and would be worth trying hard to establish. (But remember that you won't be able to call your veg 'organic' unless you have been certified by the *Soil Association*.) And also remember that it will be pretty hard work and you won't earn a fortune from it. But you will meet a lot of nice people and anyway, you don't want a fortune do you?

Minimise costs: don't buy *Mr Krunchy Oaty-Munchy*... buy a big bag of wholemeal organic porridge for a quarter of the price and twice the nourishment. Your local wholefood shop and farmers' mart should replace the supermarket for most of your necessary food shopping.

Learn new skills from evening classes, books and neighbours. Welding, carpentry, clothes repair, accountancy, wiring... anything that will help you trim unnecessary costs and which might also be a useful bartering skill.

Keep thinking...

Never let any job become automatic or routine. Keep thinking 'can I do this job better, or quicker, or can I even find a way of not needing to do it at all, possibly by better planning, or maybe by simple automation?' You could start with 'washing up', seeing as you have just passed your dishwasher on to a children's home where it can be used efficiently!

Most of us spend most of our lives in a condition scarcely differentiable from sleep. We run on rails; we live by habit; we don't think at all, if we can avoid it. If we were to wake up a smidgen and think just a little bit, we would realise that we might just as well be dead, really. We are automata.

Just as a tiny example.. Why do you use teabags (and I bet you do)? 'Because they are more convenient' of course, as the advertisers have endlessly drummed into you... but *are* they? I say No. What they actually do is to make decisions for you, cost you more, and encourage waste. Thus:

a) Trial and error has taught me that one tea bag will make at least two cups of refreshing tea. True, they will not be two cups of eye-popping, skin-crawling hi-caff, but that is not what I want from a cup of tea. Do you?

b) A teabag has been through extra and unnecessary (energy-wasting and greenhouse-gas-producing) processes. It also uses paper and possibly string and card and ink for no valuable purpose.

c) Teabags cost at least twice as much as loose tea. Check out the 'price per 100gm' tickets at the supermarket.

d) A used teabag is no use to anyone, except possibly as a coaster for an expendable sherry glass, or for tidying up a hamster with a tummy upset. Dried or semi-dried used loose leaves, however, are useful for mopping up spillage, sweeping a kitchen floor, or sticking under a cat or budgie.

e) Loose leaves will break down quicker in the compost heap.

How many other habits deserve similar analysis? I bet you could list a dozen without even trying. Go for twenty...

Think outside the box

Just because this job has always been done this way is no reason why there might not be a better way... or at least another way more suitable to your own personal circumstances. Never take anyone's word for it without thinking it through and testing it.

Rethink

...all your conventional understandings about such terms as 'happiness', 'wealth', 'enjoyment', 'worthwhile', 'status', 'value', 'self-worth', 'success', 'failure', 'tidiness', 'clothing', 'routine', 'freedom', 'poverty', 'car', 'entertainment', 'fashion', 'boring', 'creativity', 'work', 'leisure', and of course 'what life is all about'.

Take your time, and take each of these concepts one at a time, and systematically rip it to shreds: reject every conventional definition, and work out something that makes sense to *you*. Question everything. Listen to each other and your intuition. Don't be nervous. All you risk losing is a slew of stale old conventional ruts laid down by other people, not you; all you stand to gain is a clearer understanding of yourself and how you want to relate to your life and how you are going to live it from now on.

***

And once you've done all the thinking and planning and have decided to Go For It, and have finally moved into your new home...

Plan plan plan....

But don't let The Plan become a tyrant. Never be afraid to tweak it; but remember that what matters more than The Plan is that you maintain your basic self-sufficiency *principles*, whatever you may have decided they will be. If, for example, your cash crop turns out to be a big earner with a Big Future... ask yourself whether you want to return to the Big Money values of the Spurious World or stick with the more human values of the Real World.

If cash crops in general don't seem to be working, what about using some of the time you spent on them labouring for a neighbouring farmer or local builder? You'll pick up useful skills.

Prioritise

You will be constantly making decisions, as five jobs appear to suddenly need doing at once. Don't panic. Just sit down with a piece of paper and a cup of tea and work out logically which needs doing first. Perhaps some of the jobs can be done piece-meal? Perhaps something that seems urgent doesn't actually need doing at all, but is just a habit, like watching the news at six o'clock or washing the car once a week?

You will need to establish some routines, but never let them rule your life. There will be occasions when the routine should be postponed or abandoned.

Conserve your energy

On the vehicle level: never use the car for only one errand, and conversely, get out of the habit of thinking that this letter must be posted *now*, for example. When you have three, or better, five jobs to do, then go out in the car and do them, and always come back with something useful, like a sack of damaged veg from a local greengrocer, or something handy from a skip; or another big sack of amazingly nourishing and versatile porridge.

On a personal level: never go anywhere with both hands empty. Take something that needs shifting. It might be a tub of stuff for the compost heap, or a bit of ironing (ironing? ha!) that needs to go upstairs, or a book that needs putting away. Don't forget that jobs do not need to be done *now* and all at once. You can wash up a couple of items at a time (quite possibly in cold water, some of them, and without soap either), while waiting for the kettle to boil or the microwave to ping. The job might have taken all day to complete in dribs and drabs, but it *will* still have been done, and won't have taken up any of your time.

Establish sites around the house or garden where stuff-in-transit should be left. Thus, the next person going upstairs can take that book, towel, shoe as he/she passes, and nobody needs to make a special journey.

With a little such forethought and an established mind-set, you can shift amazing amounts of stuff hither and yon, more or less by accident. Just don't be in a hurry. (That's how they built the pyramids, by the way.)

Remember who you are

You are not a postman or a housewife or a nuclear engineer. You are a human being with a right and a need to be creative and live a joyful and fulfilled life. If you can agree with me that your life is a journey of self-discovery and personal evolution, take (quite a lot of) time to consider the deeper implications of this metaphor.

Treats

Rethink what a 'treat' is. In our smallholding days our treat was bacon, egg and chips at a cafe in Carmarthen once a month. Wonderful! You can keep caviar and Bolly at the Ritz twice a day.

Treats are an essential part of life, and should be planned for. And they do not need to be large; merely non-routine. (Many people are unhappy not because they haven't got enough money, but because they have too much.)

Keep a sense of proportion

...at all times in all things. If The Plan isn't working, and it can't be tweaked, then don't bust a gut pursuing failure. It didn't work... so what? Try again with a different plan which you will tailor to avoid the snags you've learned from the old plan.

What matters in your life is not 'success', but 'intelligent effort'.

If a goat/rabbit/lightning/a Russian satellite destroys all your runner beans... so what? Will you starve? No.

Remember that there will always be problems. They can't ever be entirely avoided. But what you *can* avoid is worrying about these problems. What screws people up is not problems, but worrying about them.

Also remember that the Chinese word for crisis is the same as the word for opportunity.

Laugh

...as often as possible and as loud as possible. Forget 'gritty dramas' and soaps and miserable paranoid documentaries on the telly: they are no use to you. You already know all about how ghastly the world can be. You've been there and *done* that, and quite right too. But you have no need or duty to endlessly wallow in this depressing stuff. It just drags your spirit down, and adds a little more misery to the global atmosphere.

Go for good humour wherever you might find it (and it can be hard to find on the telly, can't it, where everyone is so slick and 'ironic' and world-weary? Get selective.)

Maybe it's time to re-discover reading? Bill Bryson makes me (and millions of others) laugh a lot; Mark Twain; Alan Coren; Frank Muir; James Herriot; ask your friends for authors who amuse them.

Oh... and don't forget that news isn't 'News' unless it's bad news. Ask any journalist. No harm will come to the world if *you* give up learning 'all' about the latest atrocity in Israel/Ireland/USA/Spain/Iraq that they are lucky enough to have film of... And you personally will gain from having your paranoia-level reduced.

Try DIY: watch any Bruce Willis film, or EastBleedinEnders, but with the sound turned down. Then add your own dialogue. I promise you some magical moments.

Explore some music that you're never tried before. Have you ever heard Russian cathedral music? Tallis's Spem in Alium? Georgian folk songs? Bach's cello suites? Cajun? Bulgarian women's choirs? Jimmy Giuffre? I don't suppose any of these will actually make you laugh, but they might help lift your spirits,or encourage relaxation.

And you'll have the entire world's music to explore if you can tune into *Spotify* on your computer.

Keep a diary

A) for gardening: it is remarkable how useful it is to know what you planted last year, where, what variety, how much of it, and when. Believe me, you *will* forget, even that manic thunderstorm that washed away three oak trees, especially after five or six years.

You will learn from your notes what has grown best where

and when and quite possibly, why it did so. Conversely, what did badly and what not to repeat. If you keep notes on crop weights as well, you will be surprised at how your skills seem to effortlessly improve with the years.

B) for yourself. Video diaries are fine, but there's nothing to beat the carefully considered written word for helping you to clarify your ideas and thoughts and introspections. You can define problems wonderfully when you need to spell them onto a page; and once clearly defined, they are much easier to act upon and solve.

Become ever-more adaptable, inventive, ingenious and creative

Ours is an appallingly wasteful and thus destructive society, in which profit is the only guide to value. Thus technology de-skills people, in the interest of cheap automation and low wages. And thus we have the 'throw-away' and 'consumer' society which will ultimately waste the entire planet's resources, and pollute it into extinction in the process.

We can only reverse this trend by one person at a time having a change of heart, as you are doing...

So... reject the whole caboodle! Learn what you need to learn in order to fix things rather than junk them. This is increasingly difficult to do, I know, but I did once fix the drive on a tape-recorder with a rubber band, and a PC with a hammer. There must still be things that can be bodged, especially if you buy bodgeable goods to start with: a metal watering-can that can be soldered or welded, rather than a nasty plastic one that shatters after its first summer; shoes that will take re-soling, possibly by yourself; and never buy 'one-trip' anything. Be aware of every purchase and reject consumerist junk. Save up and buy quality.

Be observant

Experience often proves theory wrong, especially in the mysterious world of plants and animals. Get to know your land. It will vary by the yard. This bit will be good for spuds;

that bit will be awful for beans. Study what grows well and badly. Get another book on companion planting and a couple more on weeds, and stay alert. Why do docks thrive here and not there? That stray spud/pea is next to a cabbage/carrot that seems larger/smaller/spottier than the others... I wonder why? Maybe read up a bit of plant physiology, and something on the history and practice of farming.

Never be afraid to experiment

Did you know that transplanting seedlings into the same magnetic orientation as they germinated in makes for stronger plants? Despite what the 'experts' try to tell you, the world of plants remains a total mystery, very much still available to the amateur to investigate. There are thousands of discoveries just waiting to be made that might increase productivity threefold and make plants disease-proof and bug-resistant. Big Business will never do this research because their aim in life is to keep plants weak so they can sell you more chemicals. Why do you think they are pushing GM seed?

Read *The Secret Life of Plants* (Tompkins and Bird; Penguin) for sure. It's worth tracking down. You will be amazed... and inspired.

Never have a closed mind

Old wives' tales are increasingly being shown to contain substance. American homesteaders advise planting pumpkin seeds on the north-south axis. Ridiculous... but it *works*.

Never prefer theory over evidence. The only certainty about a theory is that one day it will be shown to be wrong. Trust your own experience and that of other reliable people over 'experts' every time... and never forget that the word 'expert' derives from 'ex-': a has-been, and 'spurt': a drip under pressure. A joke, obviously, but a caution nonetheless.

Never write off a technique or an approach 'because it's stupid'. The universe is most certainly stranger than your philosophy can conceive. What's more, Biodynamic Growing most definitely works, as thousands of wealthy European biodynamic farmers will attest... despite being reliant upon such 'nonsense' as the moon's phases and some extraordinarily weird concoctions. It *works.. that*'s your starting point..

You may wish to find out why... (but don't hold out any hopes of winning a Nobel Prize. You may well deserve it, and millions of gardeners will bless you for your efforts, but there are too many commercial and academic forces who will ensure that your findings remain obscure, or indeed, occult...)

Become expert at receiving advice

...but always make your own judgement. Get as much advice as you can, but remember that everyone will have different experiences, circumstances, and philosophical starting points. Some people, for example (who often like to think of themselves as 'scientists') will never admit to certain things being possible (like Biodynamics, for example.) They are not scientists at all, of course: merely bigots. This does not, of course, mean that they will never have anything of importance to say.

Always consider the person as well as the advice.

Keep on

...keeping on. You will make mistakes (so what?) and misjudgements. The secret of wisdom is to learn from your mistakes, especially if a 'mistake' could actually be a pointer to a new approach, if you but have the eyes to notice it...

And anyway... did your mistake cause your death? No, apparently not. So no harm done then... Laugh, learn, move on...

Consider all aspects

Don't just rush bull-headed at a job. Think it through in advance so you can take *all* the tools you'll need and not waste time on six trips back to the shed for the shears, sledgehammer, 9/16ths spanner and/or lemon squeezer.

While planning, make sure your timing is right. Would it be better to wait a week before putting the skin on the cloches? That way the weeds won't get such a head start, and anyway, a slightly warmer day will make the plastic more amenable, and won't be so cruel to that little gap you always seem to get between your jumper and your trousers when you bend forwards. (Good planning, of course, eventually means you no longer buy or knit short jumpers.)

And if the job is likely to involve 'waste', plan ahead for its disposal. If you're knocking down an old wall, and one day plan to have a concrete path elsewhere, try to arrange it so that you can carry the rubble and dump it in situ as hard core for the new path even if it's going to remain there waiting for a couple of years. Two birds with one stone; and lots of time and energy saved, if not today then tomorrow.

Don't rush

Speed is a false god. What *you* are looking for is effectiveness, not speed. All 'work' should be enjoyable.

Are you doing a job that you think is 'unenjoyable', and you are thus rushing to get through it? Why not start by asking 'what does 'enjoyable' mean?' Perhaps you are being blinded by convention? Perhaps shovelling cow muck is actually fun, not oh-poo-smelly? Personally, I enjoy it, as I know it is next year's fertility. No, I don't wear flip-flops, which may have something to do with it.

There are very few jobs in self-sufficiency that must be done *now*. Usually you can delay them a bit, or split them up, so that a 'boring' job becomes tolerable. But again... what *is* 'boring'? Why is weeding 200 feet of carrots 'boring'? You have a mind: exercise it while weeding; you have eyes: use them to check how each plant is looking, which insects are about, and which weeds there are in this little patch; you have ears... listen to what the local wildlife has to say, or smile at the roar of distant traffic that no longer concerns you.

...you might even take your walkman with you and learn Portuguese.

Or you might like to consider the Zen saying 'when walking, just walk', and extend it to 'when weeding, just weed.' There is no virtue in letting your mind run out of control. Switch it off now and then, and feel refreshed.

If ever you find yourself constantly rushing, just say to yourself: 'I didn't come here for this'. Rushing always means something is wrong: namely, that *you* have got something wrong. Perhaps you've not got your schedule realistically worked out; or that you've not sorted out 'repetitive' from 'boring'; or that your whole sense of values has not yet properly transferred from 'manic/distractive' to 'calm/worthwhile'. Whatever: 'rushing' means 'time to check within'.

Keep positive

Always aim to take a bright and cheery attitude with you into the garden. If that just isn't possible one rat-headed morning, then allow the calm of the plants to instil calm into you. Once that calm is securely rooted, then sort out what your problem really is. The odds are that it is not what it apparently seems to be. Go deep. Let the peace of the plants guide you.

All very airy-fairy, eh? Just try it...

An alternative approach is to learn to change your mood by an act of will. It can be done.

And yes... do talk to your plants. There have been numerous experiments that show that plants that are talked to actually *do* do better than ones that are ignored. I wonder why? And so, no doubt, do you.

Enjoyment

Never forget that what you are doing now is learning to be in charge of your own life and learning to enjoy it. In the Spurious World you've left behind, it's all about money for the sake of it, without a thought for what money *is* or why you spend half your life scrabbling round for more and more of it, and the other half of your life rushing round spending it and clearing up the mess it's left behind.

In your new world, the Real World, you will be re-defining, bit by bit, what you think your life *should* be about. You will realise for sure that such things as joy and enjoyment have nothing at all to do with money, and that your new life is not about the cost of living but about the value of life.

Sooner or later, you'll realise that some things that used to be tiresome chores are actually enjoyable and creative experiences. Fitting a new handle to a spade is something to have fun with and take pride in; laying a network of hoses; mending a torn coat; descaling the kettle with a 50/50 mix of white vinegar and water, left to soak overnight, rather than a £5.50 jar of *Deeskaylit Majic Kettle Gel (with special plastic applicator wand)*. Oh, you get the drift.

The key is time and purpose: once you stop rushing to do Spurious World things, you can slow down and enjoy the little stuff; and you will also know that doing it yourself is saving you having to spend money on it... because to get that money, you have to plunge back into the poisonous waters of Spurious World.

All your jobs in self-sufficiency should be enjoyable. They may make you tired, or be a challenge in some way, but the challenge is what you welcome. Enjoy every moment. Enjoy being tired at the end of a busy day. You'll never need another sleeping pill if you're doing the gardening right!

And finally...

It is an esoteric truth that energy follows intention and attention. Think positive, and you attract positive energies to you. If you are clear that this will be the most stimulating, exciting and positive year of your life so far... well, that is what it will become. Relish it!

Carpe diem!

Have a great day every day!

The Good Life Press Ltd.
The Old Pigsties, Clifton Fields
Lytham Road, Preston
PR4 0XG
01772 633444

The Good Life Press Ltd. is a family run business specialising in publishing a wide range of titles for the smallholder, 'goodlifer' and farmer. We also publish **Home Farmer,** the monthly magazine for anyone who wants to grab a slice of the good life - whether they live in the country or the city. Other Titles of interest:

A Guide to Traditional Pig Keeping by Carol Harris
A-Z of Practical Self-Sufficiency by Carl May
Build It! by Joe Jacobs
Build It!.....With Pallets by Joe Jacobs
Building and Using Your Clay Oven by Mike Rutland
Craft Cider Making by Andrew Lea
Flowerpot Farming by Jayne Neville
Garden Projects for Ruffians by Phil Thane
Making Country Wines, Ales and Cordials by Brian Cook
Making Jams and Preserves by Diana Sutton
No Time to Grow by Tim Wootton
Poultry Houses from Scratch by Mike Rutland
Precycle! by Paul Peacock
Raising Chickens by Mike Woolnough
Talking Sheepdogs by Derek Scrimgeour
The Bread and Butter Book by Diana Sutton
The Cheese Making Book by Paul Peacock
The Frugal Life by Piper Terrett
The Medicine Garden by Rachel Corby
The Pocket Guide to Wild Food by Paul Peacock
The Polytunnel Companion by Jayne Neville
The Sausage Book by Paul Peacock
The Secret Life of Cows by Rosamund Young
The Smoking and Curing Book by Paul Peacock
Woodburning by John Butterworth
Worms and Wormeries by Mike Woolnough

www.goodlifepress.co.uk
www.homefarmer.co.uk